Collector's Guide to

BANKS

Identification & Values

• POTTERY • PORCELAIN •
• COMPOSITION •

Beverly
&
Jim
Mangus

COLLECTOR BOOKS

A Division of Schroeder Publishing Co., Inc.

Searching For A Publisher?

We are always looking for knowledgeable people considered to be experts within their fields. If you feel that there is a real need for a book on your collectible subject and have a large comprehensive collection, contact Collector Books.

On the Cover:

Full Figure Popeye, Vandor, $100.00 – 110.00.
Padlock Pig, ABC, $350.00 – 375.00.
His and Hers Pin Money, Holt Howard, $35.00 – 40.00 each.
Farmer Pig, Treasure Craft, $75.00 – 80.00.
Ludwig Von Drake, Walt Disney, $375.00 – 400.00.

Cover Design by Beth Summers
Book Design by Karen Smith
Printed in the U.S.A. by Image Graphics Inc., Paducah KY

It is with much love we dedicate this book to our granddaughter,
Devin Elizabeth Williams.

Acknowledgments

We would like to take this opportunity to express our gratitude to the many people who helped make this book possible.

A special thank you to John and Carol Bosson, for being a part of and supporting this project from the beginning. Thank you for your friendship, for the good times, and for offering sound advice, like "just bite the bullet" and buy the bank. The memories we've made will last a lifetime.

Our sincere thanks to Jamie and Cathy Melton, for inviting us into your home, sharing your magnificent collection, and extending that gracious Southern hospitality.

To our dear friends, Charlie and Rose Snyder, we extend our gratitude once again for sharing your knowledge, expertise, and breathtaking collection, but we are most thankful for your constant love and support.

Our thanks goes out to Jeff and Judie Snyder, two of the nicest people we know, for sharing your collection and for your endless encouragement, support, and enthusiasm—and Judie's cherry pie.

We are also very grateful to the following people for providing either photographs or pieces for photography, supplying information, or helping with pricing:

Ron Brown
Christine's Unique Antique Mall, Zanesville, Ohio
Bill and Shirley Corl
Elvin Culp, Clara Belles Antiques, Zanesville, Ohio
Harvey Duke
Paul Folkers
John and Norma Grogan
Denny and Bev Huffman

Jack and Carol Jessen
Don and Margaret Merryman
Denise Teeters
Trouts Old Town Antique Mall, Zanesville, Ohio
Jerry Whetstine
Ami Williams
George Williams

Photography by Jim Mangus

CONTENTS

INTRODUCTION

As cookie jar collectors and pottery in general, we have collected banks for several years. What began as a desire to only collect banks that matched cookie jars has become the determining drive for our antiquing pursuits, searching for any rare and unusual bank.

The need for a more complete guide to Shawnee Pottery was the force that inspired us to write *Shawnee Pottery, An Identification And Price Guide,* and it was that same force, along with a lot of coaxing from other bank collectors, that brought about this book. The popularity and growth of pottery bank collecting have been overwhelming over the past three years.

Still banks have been made of many different materials, including iron, tin, pottery, glass, wood composition, chalk, and plastic. Mechanical and cast iron banks have been a popular collectible for years and there are numerous reference books about them.

To date, this is the only publication dedicated to Pottery and Porcelain banks. The difficulties have been many, and as with any uncharted territory, there is still much to be discovered.

The most notable challenge has been identification. The banks that we were able to positively identify have been placed in their appropriate places, by company name. If the bank was imported and the maker is unknown, it was placed in the section by the country from which it was imported. If we had minimal information but could not determine maker or country, we placed the bank in the Miscellaneous section. Where we had no information, we placed the bank in the Unknown section.

We have included an Index for a quick reference to every bank shown in the book, listing page, plate, company, and price of the bank. If only pricing information is what you need, you may simply refer to the Index.

The number of banks produced over the years appears endless. By the time you read this, Book II will be in progress. We will be introducing additional pottery and porcelain banks along with banks made of composition, which have not been adequately covered in this book. Unfortunately, many banks were produced with no permanent marking, and only a paper label was applied to identify the manufacturer. Maybe you have that unknown bank with the label intact! We welcome any further information you may have on the banks shown in this book and any additions that you would like to see in Book II. Please feel free to contact us: Bev & Jim Mangus, 5147 Broadway NE, Louisville, Ohio 44641.

PRICING

The prices in this book represent current market value for mint condition pieces. Banks with chips and/or hairlines will bring considerably less. Gold trimmed banks will bring approximately 40% to 50% more. As prices vary in different parts of the country according to availability, we gathered the pricing information geographically from shows, flea markets, dealers, trade papers, and collectors. The prices listed are to be used only as a guide.

Adrian Art Pottery started in Florida. It is currently operating in Roseville, Ohio, as Chrisshaun Arts.

Plate 1: Porky Crockett
Cookie jar/bank head. Marked #1 1993, Adrian Art Pottery Roseville, OH. 14½"h. $300.00 – 325.00.

Plate 2: Porky Crockett
Back view. Artist signed, F. Ault Moore.

Plate 3: Pig with Pacifier
Cookie jar/bank head. Marked with ink stamp "Adrian Art Pottery, Roseville, OH." 11"h. $175.00 – 200.00

Plate 4: Model T Cookie Jar/Bank
Signed "F.O. Moore Chrisshaun Arts, Adrian Art, Roseville, OH." 11"h. $250.00 – 275.00.

Plate 5: Model T
Front view of Model T.

7

American Bisque Company, (ABC) Williamstown, West Virginia, 1919 – 1982
American Pottery Company, (APCO) Marietta, Ohio, 1944 – 1965

Some of the most sought after banks by today's collectors were produced by these two companies. We have chosen to combine the two companies because of their compact association.

For a number of years, the American Pottery Company was co-owned by A.N. Allen and J.B. Lenhart. Allen was also the sole owner of The American Bisque Pottery Company where J.B. Lenhart worked as a sales manager. Because of these close connections, we get an interchange of products between the two companies.

The American Bisque Pottery Company began making figural character pieces in 1937 and continued until the company was sold. The cartoon characters are among the most popular banks.

American Bisque Pottery is often identified by wedges on the bottom of the piece. However, both American Bisque and American Pottery banks can be found with flat bottoms, outline footing, circular footing and U-shaped footing. The banks that we have confirmed (ABC) or (APCO) have been marked as such next to the name. The Disney Banks that American Bisque made for the Leeds China Company can be found in the Walt Disney section.

The Boy and Girl Pig Wall Hanging Banks were produced in several color variations and were originally advertised as Wall Pin-Up Banks.

Plate 6: Betty (ABC)
Name is reference given by collectors.
12¾"h x 6"w. Marked "USA 662." $500.00+.

Plate 7: Floyd (ABC)
Name is reference given by collectors.
12¾"h x 6"w. Marked "USA 661." $500.00+.

Plate 8: For Your Rainy Day
Marked "USA." 6¼"hx7½"l. $200.00 – 250.00.

Plate 9: For Your Rainy Day
Color variation. $125.00 – 150.00.

Plate 10: For Your Rainy Day
Color variation. $125.00 – 150.00.

Plate 11: For Your Rainy Day
Color variation. $125.00 – 150.00.

Plate 12: Tic Tac Toe Kitten
Unmarked. 5"h. $75.00 – 85.00.

Plate 13: Tic Tac Toe Kitten
Color variation. $75.00 – 85.00.

9

Plate 14: Fluffy Cat (APCO)
Unmarked. 9½"h. $40.00 – 45.00.

Plate 15: Fluffy Cat (APCO)
Unmarked. 5¾"h. Gold trim.
$40.00 – 45.00.

Plate 16: Fluffy Cat (APCO)
Color variation. $40.00 – 45.00.

Plate 17: Fluffy Cat (APCO)
Color variation. $40.00 – 45.00.

Plate 18: Feed the Kitty
Marble eyes. Marked "USA."
Kitty (left), 8"h. $95.00 – 100.00.
Kitty (right), 7"h. $95.00 – 100.00.

Plate 19: Figaro
Unmarked. 6¾"h. $100.00 – 125.00.

Plate 20: Mr. Pig (APCO)
Feet together. Unmarked. 6"h.
$35.00 – 40.00.

Plate 21: Mr. Pig
Color variation.
$35.00 – 40.00.

Plate 22: Mr. Pig (APCO)
Feet apart. Unmarked. 6"h.
$35.00 – 40.00.

Plate 23: Mr. Pig
Feet apart. Color variation.
$35.00 – 40.00.

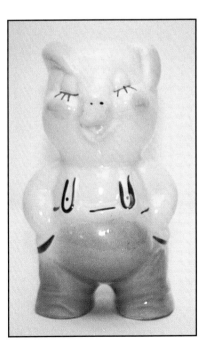

Plate 24: Mr. Pig
Feet apart. Color variation.
$35.00. – 40.00.

Plate 25: Pig with Bow (APCO)
Cold paint. Unmarked. 6"h. $35.00 – 40.00 each.

Plate 26: Fatsy (APCO)
Recessed eyes. Marked "Fatsy USA."
5¾"h. $75.00 – 80.00.

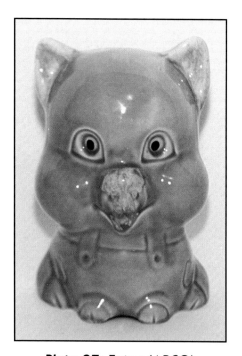

Plate 27: Fatsy (APCO)
Color variation. $75.00 – 80.00.

Plate 28: Fatsy (APCO)
Color variation. $75.00 – 80.00.

Plate 29: Fatsy (APCO)
Eyes are not recessed. Marked "Fatsy
USA." 5¾"h. $75.00 – 80.00.

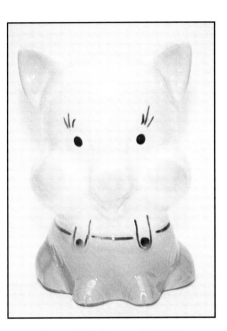

Plate 30: Fatsy (APCO)
Color variation. $75.00 – 80.00.

Plate 31: Fatsy (APCO)
Fatsy (left), recessed eyes. 5¾"h. $75.00 – 85.00.
Fatsy (right), smaller version without recessed eyes. 4½"h. $85.00 – 95.00.

Plate 32: Puppy (APCO)
Blue puppy, marked, "USA." 3¾"h; Brown puppy, marked "USA." 3¾"h;
Yellow puppy, unmarked. 3½"h. $30.00 – 35.00 each.

Plate 33: Puppy (APCO)
Bottom of puppy banks showing two different bottoms.

Plate 34: Spaniel with Basket (APCO)
Marked "USA." 6"h. $45.00 – 50.00.

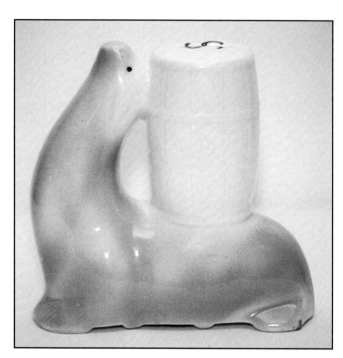

Plate 35: Seal with Barrel
Unmarked. 5¾"h. $45.00 – 50.00.

Plate 36: Fish (ABC)
Marked "USA." 6"h. $45.00 – 50.00.

Plate 37: Swan (ABC)
Gold trim. Marked "USA." 3¼"h. $45.00 – 50.00.

Sweet Pea is probably most sought after by bank collectors. Do not confuse the American Bisque Sweet Pea with the Vandor Sweet Pea, (shown in the Vandor section) which is much smaller and lighter in weight.

Plate 38: Sweet Pea
Unmarked. 6¼"h. $1,500.00+.

Plate 39: Sweet Pea
Side view.

Plate 40: Popeye
Unmarked. 7"h. $475.00 – 500.00.

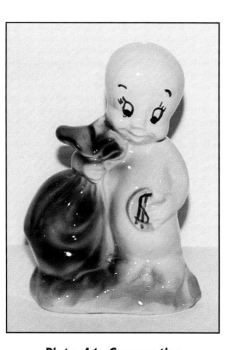

Plate 41: Casper the Friendly Ghost
Marked "USA." 8½"h. $450.00 – 475.00.

Plate 42: Little Audrey
Unmarked. 8½"h. $600.00 – 625.00.

Plate 43: Little Audrey
Side view.

Plate 44: Dino
Unmarked except for incised "Dino." 8½"h. $525.00 – 550.00.

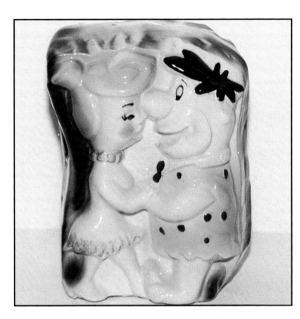

Plate 45: Fred Loves Wilma
Unmarked except for the inscription "Fred Loves Wilma" in the heart. 8½"h. $400.00 – 425.00. Note: Beware of the reproduction! The glaze colors are slightly different, and the decorating is poorly done.

The Boy/Girl Turnabout was also made as a cookie jar and cookie jar with bank slot in the lid. This bank however, is all one piece and is not the cookie jar with fused-on lid.

Plate 46: Boy/Girl Turnabout (APCO)
Sad girl view. Gold trim. Unmarked. 9"h. $200.00 – 225.00.

Plate 47: Boy/Girl Turnabout (APCO)
Happy boy side.

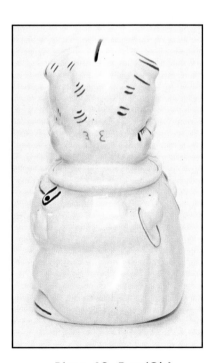

Plate 48: Boy/Girl Turnabout (APCO)
Side view.

Plate 49: Padlock Pig
Marked "USA 912." 10½"h. $475.00 – 500.00.
Coins are removed through the lid that is
held in place by a tiny padlock.

Plate 50: Diaper Pin Pig
Gold trim. Marked "USA." 9"h. $350.00 – 375.00.

Plate 51: Roy Rogers and Trigger
Unmarked except for Roy Rogers and Trigger in
raised letters. 7½"h. $300.00 – 325.00.

Plate 52: Tepee and Indian Boy
Unmarked. 7¼"h. Dark faced boy, $65.00 – 75.00;
light faced boy, $65.00 – 75.00.

Plate 53: Jalopy (ABC)
Marked "USA." 4½"h. $65.00 – 75.00.

Plate 56: Humpty Dumpty
Advertising piece. Marked "Alice In Philcoland." 6"h. $120.00 – 130.00.

Plate 54: Girl and Boy Yarn Doll
Unmarked. 5¼"h. $60.00 – 65.00 each.

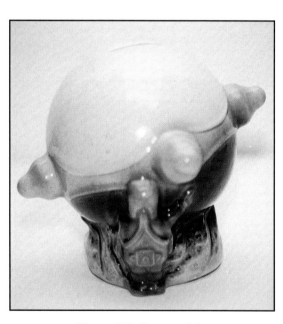

Plate 57: Spaceship
Marked "USA." 5½"h. $75.00 – 80.00.

Plate 55: Boy and Girl Yarn Doll
Color variation. $60.00 – 65.00 each.

Plate 58: Happy Elephant
Gold trim. Unmarked. 5"h. $55.00 – 60.00.

Plate 59: Happy Elephant
Color variation. $40.00 – 45.00.

Plate 60: Sitting Polar Bear
Color variation. Gold trim.
$40.00 – 45.00.

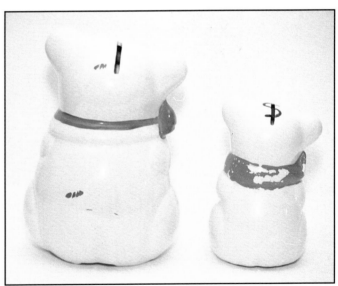

Plate 61: Sitting Polar Bears (APCO)
Unmarked. Large, 8"h. $50.00 – 55.00;
small 5¾"h. $25.00 – 35.00.

Plate 62: Sitting Polar Bears (APCO)
View of back.

Plate 63: Lamb
Cold paint. Unmarked. 6¼"h.
$25.00 – 30.00.

Plate 64: Sitting Teddy Bear (APCO)
Unmarked. Large, 12"h. $55.00 – 65.00;
small, 6¾"h. $25.00 – 30.00.

Plate 65: Sitting Teddy Bear
Color variation. $40.00 – 45.00.

Plate 66: Stuffed Bear
Unmarked. 5"h. $40.00 – 45.00.

Plate 67: Standing Elephant on Base
Two color variations. Unmarked. 6"h. $55.00 – 65.00 each.

Plate 68: Dancing Elephant on Base
Unmarked. 6"h $65.00 – 75.00.

Plate 69: Squirrel with Nut on Base
Unmarked. 6½"h. $45.00 – 50.00.

Plate 70: Squirrel with Nut on Base
Color variation. $45.00 – 50.00.

**Plate 71: Upside Down
Pig on Base**
Unmarked. 6"h. $65.00 – 70.00.

Plate 72: Donkey on Base
Unmarked. 6"h. $65.00 – 70.00.

Plate 73: Little Girl Pig (APCO)
Gold trim. Marked "USA" with a paper
label. 5¾"h. $40.00 – 45.00.

**Plate 74: Little Girl
Pig (APCO)**
Side view.

**Plate 75: Indented Dot
Dancing Pig**
Unmarked. 4¾"h. $30.00 – 35.00.

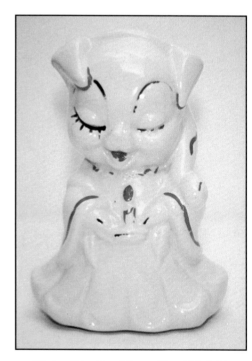

Plate 76: Bedtime Pig (APCO)
Flared dress. Cold paint. Marked "USA."
6½"h. $30.00 – 35.00.

Plate 77: Bedtime Pig
Slightly different mold, dress not
flared. Unmarked. 5¾"h. Gold trim.
$35.00 – 40.00.

Plate 78: Bedtime Pig
Color variation. $35.00 – 40.00.

Plate 79: Dimples
Cold paint. Unmarked. 6"h. $30.00 – 35.00.

Plate 80: Dimples
Color variation. $35.00 – 40.00.

Plate 81: Bow Pig
Marked "USA." 5½"h. $30.00 – 35.00.

Plate 82: Bow Pigs
Two different variations. Left, 5½"h. Marked "USA." Right, 5¼"h.
Marked "USA." $30.00 – 35.00 each.

Plate 83: Bow Pig
Mold variation. Marked "USA."
5¼"h. $35.00 – 40.00.

Plate 84: Bow Pig
Color variation and open eyes.
$30.00 – 35.00.

Plate 85: Pig with Bow (APCO)
Unmarked. 4"h. $30.00 – 35.00.

Plate 86: Elephant
Unmarked. 5¾"h. $30.00 – 35.00.

Plate 87: Chick
Unmarked. 6½"h. $45.00 – 50.00.

Plate 88: Squirrel
Unmarked. 5½"h. $25.00 – 30.00.

Plate 89: Snowmen
Color variations. Unmarked. 6½"h. $65.00 – 70.00.

Plate 90: Snowman
View of back. "Tommy Ray" is written
on back of center Snowman.

Plate 91: Santa
Unmarked. 3¾"h. $90.00 – 100.00.

Plate 92: Apple Wallhanger
Unmarked. 3"h. $25.00 – 30.00.

Plate 93: Telephone
Unmarked. 5¾"h. $30.00 – 35.00.

Paddy Pig is shown with a cork in the top of the hat. The cork is not the correct stopper; the stopper should be a piece resembling the crown of the hat with a feather in it. The crown is removed to retrieve the coins.

Plate 95: Standing Pig
Embossed clover. Marked "USA" under the chin.
6¼"hx14"l. $100.00 – 110.00.

Plate 94: Paddy Pig
Marked "APCO 1958 USA." 6"hx6"l. $70.00 – 75.00.

Plate 96: Standing Pig
Recessed petals. Unmarked. 4½"hx7¼"l.
$45.00 – 50.00.

Plate 97: Standing Pig
Embossed flowers. Marked "USA" under the chin.
7"hx12½"l. $100.00 – 110.00.

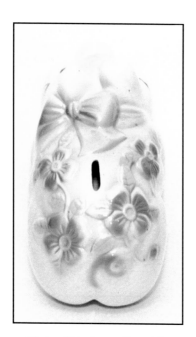

Plate 98: Standing Pig
Top view of the Standing Pig
with embossed flowers.

Plate 99: Standing Pig
Marked "USA" on base of foot. 4½"hx7"l. $45.00 – 50.00.

Plate 100: Attitude Pig with Bow
Cold paint. Slot on hip. Marked "USA." 7'hx12½"l. $50.00 – 55.00.

Plate 101: Attitude Pig with Bow
Marked "USA." 8½"hx13'l. $100.00 – 110.00.

Plate 102: Attitude Pig with Bow
Top view.

Plate 103: Attitude Pig with Bow
For a new car. Marked "USA." 6¼"hx12"l. $110.00 – 120.00.

Plate 104: Attitude Pig with Bow
Marked "USA." 5½"hx7½"l. $85.00 – 90.00.

Plate 105: Two Small Attitude Pigs
Unmarked. 3¼"hx4½"l.
$25.00 – 30.00 each.

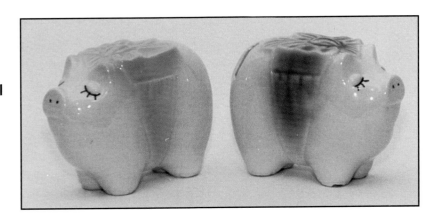

Plate 106: Attitude Pig with Recessed Cloverleaf
Marked "USA." 6"hx8"l. $85.00 – 90.00.

Plate 107: Attitude Pig
Marked "USA." 6"hx8"l. $70.00 – 75.00.

Plate 108: Standing Pig with Bow
Marked "USA." 5¼"hx7"l. $55.00 – 65.00.

Plate 109: Standing Pig with Bow
Marked "USA." 5¾"hx7½"l. $45.00 – 50.00.

Plate 110: Standing Pig with Indented Dots
Unmarked. 7½"hx13"l. $100.00 – 110.00.

Plate 111: Standing Pig with Indented Dots
Unmarked. 5¼"hx7½"l. $30.00 – 35.00.

Plate 112: Standing Pig with Indented Dots
Unmarked. 3"hx6"l. $30.00 – 35.00.

Plate 113: Pig with Embossed Flower
Cold paint and open eyes. Unmarked.
4¼"hx7"l. $25.00 – 30.00.

Plate 114: Hands in the Pocket Pig Turnabout
Cookie jar/bank head. Marked "USA."
10¼"h. $250.00 – 300.00.

Plate 115: Hands In the Pocket Pig Turnabout
Reverse side.

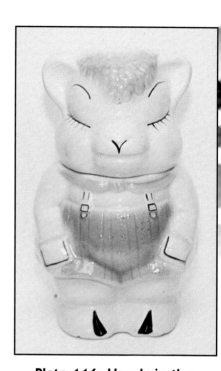

Plate 116: Hands in the Pocket Lamb/Bull Turnabout
Cookie jar/bank head. Unmarked.
10¼"h. $250.00 – 300.00.

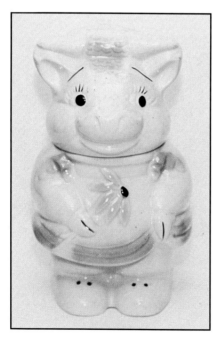

Plate 117: Hands in the Pocket Lamb/Bull Turnabout
Reverse side.

Plate 118: Hands in the Pocket Pig
Cookie jar/bank head. Unmarked. 10½"h.
$250.00 – 300.00.

Applause, an importer/distributor, importing primarily from Taiwan and China. Applause is best known for its licensed pieces.

Plate 119: Woody Woodpecker
Paper label "1957 Walter Lantz; Applause Inc.
Woodland Hills, Ca. 91367; Made in Taiwan Item
26405." 6¾"h. $55.00 – 60.00.

Plate 120: Annie
Paper label "Applause; ™Knickerbocker Toy Co.; Middlesex, NJ;
© 1982 Columbia Picture Ind.; © 1982 Tribune Company Syndicate, Inc.; Item 8906." 5¾"h. $65.00 – 70.00.

Plate 121: Felix the Cat
Paper label "Applause, Inc.; 1989 Felix the Cat Productions; Made in Taiwan; Sku 26542."
Sitting Felix, 5¾"h. $45.00 – 50.00. Standing Felix, 7"h. $45.00 – 50.00.

Plate 122: Ernie in Train
Marked "Jim Henson Productions, Inc." 4"h. $30.00 – 35.00.

Plate 123: Cookie Monster
Marked "©Jim Henson Productions, Inc."
5¾"h. $30.00 – 35.00.

Plate 124: Big Bird with Toy Chest
Marked "©Jim Henson Productions, Inc."
Paper label "Applause, Inc." 4½"h. $30.00 – 35.00.

Plate 125: Lion
Marked "©Atlantic Mold" and the initials,
"KC WAS" on foot. 8¼"h. $20.00 – 25.00.

Beaumont Bros. Pottery

Currently located in Crooksville, Ohio. Beaumont Brothers Pottery is best known for their Early American salt glaze and spongeware. Each piece is marked with the initials BBP and with the year manufactured.

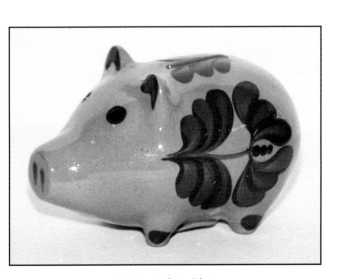

Plate 126: Pig
Marked "BBP 1993." 3½"h. $15.00 – 18.00.

Plate 127: Rabbit
Marked "BBP 1993."
7"h. $15.00 – 18.00.

BENJAMIN & MEDWIN, INC.

Benjamin & Medwin, a New York based importer/distributor. Specializing in licensed items.

Plate 128: Ernie the Keebler Elf
Marked "1989 Keebler Comp."
8½"h. $40.00 – 45.00.

Plate 129: Blue Bonnet Sue
Marked "1989 Nabisco."
8"h. $30.00 – 35.00.

Plate 130: Pillsbury Dough Boy
Marked "1988 The Pillsbury Company."
8"h. $25.00 – 30.00.

BLUE MOUNTAIN POTTERY

Plate 131: Bear
Unmarked. 6"h. $65.00 – 70.00.

Brush Pottery began operations in 1909. When George S. Brush joined the J.W. McCoy Pottery Company it was renamed Brush-McCoy Pottery. In 1925 Brush-McCoy was renamed Brush Pottery. The company closed in 1982. Brush is most known for its cookie jars, lawn ornaments, and planters.

Plate 132: Sitting Pig
Fashioned after the cookie jar. Production 1965.
Marked "837 USA Brush." 10½"h. $400.00 – 450.00.

Plate 133: Formal Pig
Two color variations. Production 1954.
Marked "W-7 USA." 11¼"h. $300.00 – 350.00 each.

Plate 134: Clown
This is a cookie jar with a bank slot in top of hat. Production 1970. Unmarked. 10¾"h. $300.00 – 350.00.

Plate 135: Standing Pig
Productions 1959. Unmarked. 5"hx7½"l. $55.00 – 60.00.

Plate 136: Small Standing Pig
Production 1952. Marked "USA." 3¾"h. $30.00 – 35.00.

Plate 137: Standing Pig
Two color variations.

Plate 138: Small Standing Pig
Color variation.

Plate 139: Razor Back Pig
Unmarked. Cold paint. 4½"hx7"l. $40.00 – 45.00.

Plate 140: Razor Back Pig Bank and Lamp
Unmarked. 4½"h. $75.00 – 80.00.

Plate 141: Standing Pig
Unmarked. 3½"h. $30.00 – 35.00.

Plate 142: Camel
Production 1940. Unmarked. 5"h. $70.00 – 75.00.

Plate 143: Dog
Unmarked. 6"h. $45.00 – 50.00.

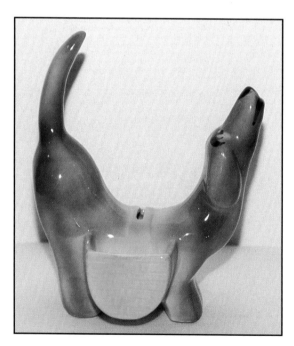

Plate 144: Rover
Marked "Rover." 8½"l. $30.00 – 35.00.

Plate 145: Monkey
Unmarked. 4½"h. $65.00 – 70.00.

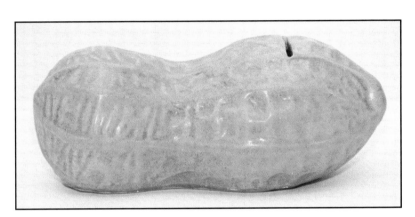

Plate 146: Peanut
Wall hanger. Unmarked. 7½"l. $60.00 – 65.00.

Plate 147: Hobo
Production 1915. Unmarked.
5¼"h. $75.00 – 80.00.

Plate 148: Brownie
Production 1968. Marked "®Brownie Gold."
6¼"h. $65.00 – 70.00.

Plate 149: Standing Pig
Unmarked. 3"hx5"l. $40.00 – 45.00.

Plate 150: Lion
Also available in orange. Unmarked. 4½"hx10"l. $110.00 – 125.00.

Plate 151: Stylized Owl
Unmarked. Two series of 25 pieces each produced with one series numbered 1–25 on back of head. 6½"h. $200.00 – 225.00.

Plate 152: Stylized Frog
Unmarked except "Albert," under the glaze.
9¼"h. $150.00 – 160.00.

Plate 153: Owls
Unmarked. 9¼"h. $75.00 – 80.00 each.

California Originals was located in Torrence, California, from 1944 to 1982. This company started as Heirlooms of Tomorrow in 1944, manufacturing Dresden lace figurines (porcelain pieces decorated with applied lace and roses). The name was changed to California Originals in 1955 and the product line was changed to items such as cookie jars, salt and peppers, planters, figurines, and banks. California Originals had contracts with Disney and Sesame Street, producing the wonderful character banks so sought after by today's collectors.

Plate 154: Soldier
Marked "USA." 7¼"h. $55.00 – 60.00.

Plate 155: Squirrel
Marked "471 USA." 7½"h. $55.00 – 60.00

Plate 156: Poodle
Marked "470 USA." 7"hx11"l. $90.00 – 95.00.

Plate 157: Sheriff with Hole in Hat
Unmarked. 12"h. $55.00 – 60.00.

CAMARK POTTERY, INC.

Camark Pottery began as Camark Art and Tile Pottery in 1926 in Camden, Arkansas. The company was sold in 1928 and the name was changed to Camark Art Pottery. The competitive import market forced the sale of the company once again in 1962. At that time the name was changed to Camark Pottery, Inc. and remained so until its closing in 1982. In 1986 the remaining stock was purchased and an attempt to recommence pottery production was made, to no avail.

Plate 158: Man
Wall hanger bank. Marked "USA Camark 247." 4½"h. $55.00 – 60.00.

CANUCK POTTERY

A Canada based company.

Plate 159: Owl
Paper label "Canuck Pottery, Quebec Ltd. Laselle, Made in Canada." 6¼"h. $25.00 – 30.00.

Cardinal China Co.

The Cardinal China Company was a distributor located in Carteret, New Jersey, with their wares being produced primarily in Hong Kong, Taiwan, and the Philippines.

Plate 160: Soldier
Cookie jar/bank head. Marked
"312 USA Cardinal." 12½"h.
$500.00 – 550.00.

Chic Pottery

Chic Pottery started in the late 1930s and remained in operation until the mid 1950s. It was located in Wellsville, Ohio, and later in Zanesville, Ohio. Chic Pottery often used delicate decals and gold trim. Many pieces are marked with an ink stamp and dated.

Plate 161: Sitting Pig
Marked with an ink stamp
"1948 Chic Pottery Co.©."
9"h. $75.00 – 80.00.

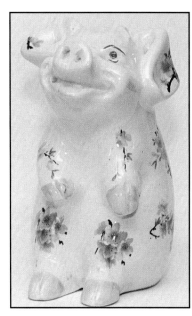

Plate 162: Sitting Pig
Unmarked. 7"h.
$70.00 – 75.00.

Plate 163: Sitting Pig
Marked with a gold ink stamp "1948
Chic Pottery Co.©." 6¾"h.
$70.00 – 75.00.

Plate 164: Sitting Pig
Marked with an ink stamp "1943 Chic
Pottery Co.©." 7"h. $75.00 – 80.00.

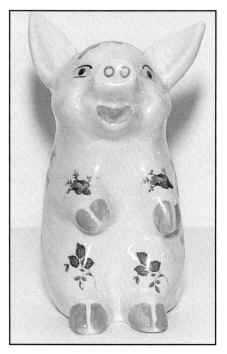

Plate 165: Sitting Pig
Marked with an ink stamp "1943 Chic
Pottery Co.©." $85.00 – 90.00.

Plate 166: Standing Pig with Seven Piglets
Standing pig, 2½"hx4½"l; piglets ½"hx1"l. Unmarked. $125.00 – 130.00 set.

The California Cleminsons was a family-owned company which began in El Monte, California, in 1941. By 1963 George and Betty Cleminson were unable to compete with the Japanese imported pottery. Rather than cheapen their wares, they decided to close their doors.

Plate 167: Jalopy
Marked with an ink stamp "The California Cleminsons." 3¾"h.
$35.00 – 40.00.

CORL POTTERY CO.

The Corl Pottery Company is owned by Shirley Corl and is located in Caro, Michigan. Shirley does all her own designs and each piece is hand decorated. Corl Pottery is best known for its limited edition cookie jars. The Humpty Dumpty Bank is an extension of the quality that we have come to expect from The Corl Pottery Company.

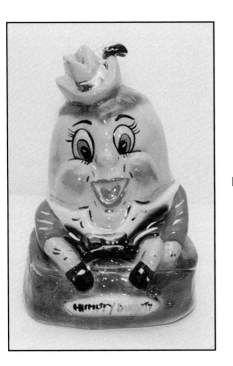

Plate 168: Humpty Dumpty
Marked "Corl Pottery Co. Limited Edition USA 1995 10/50" (indicating that only 50 of these banks were produced). 6¾"h.
$80.00 – 85.00.

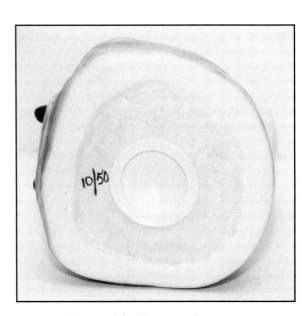

Plate 169: Humpty Dumpty
View of bottom.

DeForest of California

DeForest was another family-owned California pottery company. It was in operation from 1950 to 1970.

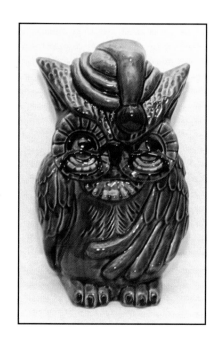

Plate 170: Owl
Marked "DeForest of Calif.
USA." 12¾"h. $35.00 – 40.00.

Diamond Pottery Corp.

The Diamond Pottery Company started out as Diamond Stoneware in Crooksville, Ohio, from 1892 – 1945. In 1945 it became the Diamond Novelty Company and later the Diamond Pottery Corporation and went from producing utilitarian pieces to decorative items until 1959. At that time it was sold to the Knight Brothers, and by 1970 it was the home of Spring Lumber Company.

Plate 171: Donkey
Paper label "Diamond Pottery Corp." 7¼"h.
$35.00 – 40.00.

Plate 172: Chick
Paper label "Rempl BN ERprises Diamond Pottery Corp." 5¼"h. $35.00 – 40.00.

Enesco is a distributor based in Elk Grove Village, Illinois. Most of its products are imported from Japan and more recently, China and Indonesia. The Disney banks by Enesco can be found in the Walt Disney section.

Plate 173: Lion (from the Wizard of Oz)
Paper label "© 1939 Loew's Incorporated, 1966; Metro Goldwyn-Mayor, Inc.; 1988 Turner Entertainment Co.; Licensee Enesco Imports Corp." A second paper label "Enesco 1989 Enesco Imports Corp.; Made in Taiwan R.O.C." 5¼"h. $75.00 – 80.00.

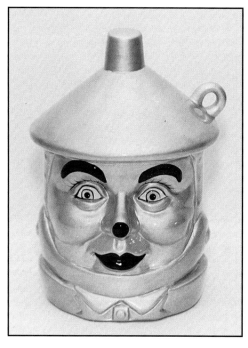

Plate 174: Tinman (from the Wizard of Oz)
Marked the same as the Lion (at left). 6¾"h. $75.00 – 80.00.

Plate 175: Scarecrow (from the Wizard of Oz)
Marked the same as the Lion (above left). 6¾"h. $75.00 – 80.00.

Plate 176: Human Bean Holding Money Bag
Paper label "Human Beans © 1981 Morgan Inc. Lic.
Enesco Imports." 5¾"h. $35.00 – 40.00.

Plate 177: Human Bean Sunbathing
Paper label "Human Beans 1981 Morgan Inc. Lic. Enesco
Imports." 4¾"h. $35.00 – 40.00.

Plate 178: Human Bean with Tennis Racket
Paper label "Human Beans © 1981 Morgan Inc. Lic.
Enesco Imports." 6¼"h. $35.00 – 40.00.

Plate 179: Human Bean with Bowling Ball
Paper label "Human Beans 1981 Morgan Inc. Lic.
Enesco Imports." 5½"h. $35.00 – 40.00.

Plate 180: Human Bean with Money
Paper label "Human Beans 1981 Morgan Inc.
Lic. Enesco Imports."
5½"h. $35.00 – 40.00.

Plate 181: Human Bean with Skis
Paper label "Human Beans 1981 Morgan Inc.
Lic. Enesco Imports."
7¼"h. $35.00 – 40.00.

**Plate 182: Human Bean,
Need Christmas Cash**
Paper label "I'm a Human Bean." 5"h. $50.00 –
55.00.

Plate 183: Human Santa Bean and Baby Bean
Paper label "Enesco." 5"h. $65.00 – 70.00.

**Plate 184: Human Bean Sunbathing
with Newspaper**
Marked with a stamp "1983 Morgan Inc. Lic.
Enesco Imports." 4¾"h. $35.00 – 40.00.

Plate 185: Human Bean with Ball Bat
Paper label "Human Beans 1981 Morgan
Inc. Lic. Enesco Imports." 6¼"h.
$35.00 – 40.00.

Plate 186: Clown
Paper label "Enesco." 7"h.
$20.00 – 25.00.

Plate 187: Jimmy Blooper
Paper label "Enesco Sports Skwirts 1979."
6¾"h. $35.00 – 40.00.

Plate 188: Sitting Unicorn and Standing Giraffe
Paper label "Enesco." Each 6½"h. $25.00 – 30.00.

Plate 189: Precious Moments Standing Pig
Paper label "Enesco Designed Giftware."
5"h. $15.00 – 20.00.

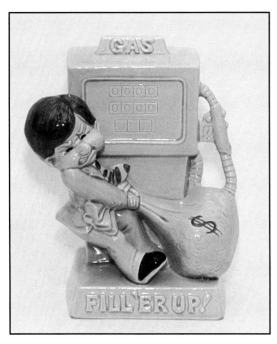

Plate 190: Gas Pump, Fill 'Er Up
Marked with a stamp "Enesco 1979 E-3519."
Signed "MR." 6¼"h. $25.00 – 30.00.

Plate 191: Santa's Toy Shop
Paper label "Enesco." 5½"h. $35.00 – 40.00.

Plate 192: Superman
Paper label "Enesco © 1987 Enesco Imports Corp. Made in Taiwan R.O.C." 6¼"h. $100.00 – 110.00.

Plate 193: Clown Head
Paper label "© 1977 Annette Little Enesco Import Corp." 6½"h. $30.00 – 35.00.

Plate 194: Elmo in Train
Marked "1993 © Jim Henson Productions, Inc. Licensee Enesco Corporation." 5¾"h. $45.00 – 50.00.

Plate 195: Elmo
Paper label "Sesame Street; 1994 Jim Henson Productions, Inc.; Licensee Enesco Corporation." 5"h. $45.00 – 50.00.

Plate 196: Big Bird in Car
Marked "1993 © Jim Henson Productions, Inc.; Licensee
Enesco Corporation; Made in China." 6½"h. $45.00 – 50.00.

Plate 197: Standing Garfield
Paper label "1978 – 1981 United Feature Syndicate;
Licensee Enesco." 7"h. $45.00 – 50.00.

Plate 198: Sitting Garfield
Paper label "1978 – 1981 United Feature Syndicate
Licensee Enesco. 4¾"h. $45.00 – 50.00.

Plate 199: Garfield with Arms Crossed
Paper label "Garfield by Jim Davis 1978 – 1981
United Feature Syndicate Licensee Enesco."
6'h. $50.00 – 55.00.

Plate 200: Mother's Pin Money
Paper label "Imports Enesco Japan."
5¾"h. $200.00 – 210.00

Plate 201: House with Bear
Paper label "Enesco." $25.00 – 30.00.

Plate 202: Speedboat
Paper label "1991 Enesco Corporation by David Olsen."
3¾"h. $25.00 – 30.00.

Plate 203: Taxi
Paper label "1991 Enesco Corporation by David Olsen."
3½"h. $35.00 – 40.00.

Plate 204: Standing Pig (October)
Stamped "Precious Moments 1988
Samuel J. Butcher." 3"h. $15.00 – 20.00.

Plate 205: Milk Money Cow
Unmarked, would have had a paper label.
5"h. $20.00 – 22.00.

Plate 206: Poodle
Stamped "Enesco." 6¼"h. $45.00 – 50.00.

Plate 207: Standing Pig
Unmarked Signature Series. 8"h x 11½"l. $90.00 – 95.00.

Plate 208: Egg-Stinct-O'Saurs
Head comes off to retrieve coins. Paper label "Egg-Stinct-O'Saurs,
1987 Enesco Imports Corp." 6½"l. $30.00 – 35.00.

Fitz and Floyd is a distributor based in Dallas, Texas, founded in 1960 by Pat Fitzpatrick and Bob Floyd. In today's market Fitz and Floyd is considered a leader in high quality dinnerware, giftware, and decorative accessories.

Plate 209: Rolls Royce
Marked, "Fitz and Floyd Inc. © MCMLXXIII FF." Paper label "FF Japan."
5"h x 8¼"l. $80.00 – 85.00.

Plate 210: Airplane
Marked "Fitz and Floyd Inc. © MCMLXXVIII." 5¾"hx 9"l. $80.00 – 85.00.

Plate 211: Boxing Kangaroo
Marked "© FF 1980." 6¾"h. $60.00 – 65.00.

Plate 212: Platypus
Marked "Fitz and Floyd Inc. © MCMLXXX 1980." 5"h.
$45.00 – 50.00.

Plate 213: Cheshire Cat
Marked "© FF 1992." 5¼"h x 7"l. $55.00 – 60.00.

Plate 214: Dracula
Marked "© FF." 6½"h. $130.00 – 135.00.

Plate 215: Hampshire Hog
Marked "© FF". 6¾"h. $55.00 – 60.00.

Frankoma Pottery is currently in operation in Sapula, Oklahoma.

Plate 216: Running Pig
Paper label "Original Creations by
Frankoma." 4¼"h. $40.00 – 45.00.

Believed to be a California based company.

Plate 217: Bear
Marked "Rita Hawkins."
7"h. $45.00 – 50.00.

Plate 218: Bear
Marked "L505." 7"h. $45.00 – 50.00.

Plate 219: Bear
Color variation. $45.00 – 50.00.

GOEBEL ART

Plate 220: Monk
Marked "5D29 Goebel W. Germany."
4½"h. $45.00 – 50.00.

Plate 221: Owl
Marked "50 076-75 Goebel W. Germany." 5½"h. $45.00 – 50.00.

Plate 222: Squirrel
Marked "5005 Goebel W. Germany." 4¾"h. $65.00 – 70.00.

Plate 223: Whale
Marked "50 08616 Goebel W. Germany." 6½"h. $65.00 – 70.00.

Plate 224: Bluebird
Marked "5 003010 Goebel W. Germany." 4¾"h. $65.00 – 70.00.

Plate 225: Bear
Marked "Goebel West Germany." 5¾"h.
$65.00 – 70.00.

Plate 226: Mouse on a Slipper
Marked "50-075-73 Goebel W. Germany." 5½"h. $75.00 – 80.00.

GONDER ART POTTERY

Gonder Art Pottery was located in Zanesville, Ohio, from 1941 to 1957. Due to the competition of foreign imports, it was forced to change its production line to tile in 1955.

Plate 227: Sheriff
Marked "Gonder." 9½"h. $550.00 – 575.00.

Plate 228: Sheriff
Color variation. 9½"h. $550.00 – 575.00.

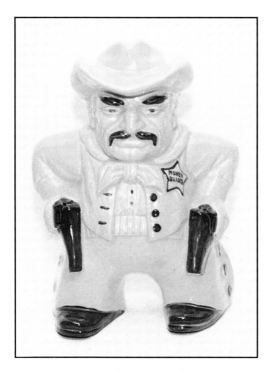

Plate 229: Sheriff
Color variation. $550.00 – 575.00.

Plate 230: Sheriff
Sheriff cookie jar with bank slot
Unmarked. 11"h. $800.00 – 850.00.

Holt Howard

Plate 231: Lion (Nodder)
Marked "Holt Howard." 6"h. $70.00 – 75.00.

Plate 232: His and Hers Pin Money
Marked "Holt Howard." 4¼"h. $35.00 – 40.00 each.

Plate 233: Cat (Two Sided)
Marked "Holt Howard." 4¼"h. $70.00 – 75.00.

Plate 234: Cat (Two Sided)
Back view of Cat.

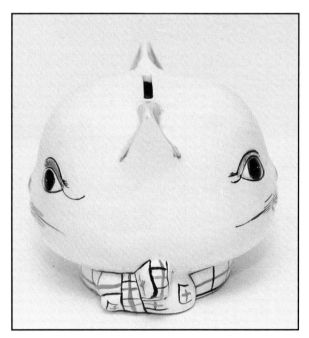

Plate 235: Cat (Two Sided)
Side view of Cat.

Hull Pottery was located in Crooksville, Ohio, from 1905 to 1985. Hull is best known for its pastel matte finished art pottery, Little Red Riding Hood, and of course, its Corky Pig banks.

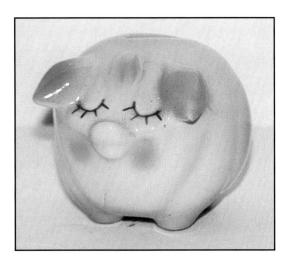

Plate 236: Standing Pig, Dime Bank
Marked "USA HP 58 ©." 3¼"h"x4¾"l. $200.00 – 225.00.

Plate 237: Dime Banks
Three color variations. The bank on the left is the same as the bank shown in Plate 236.
The center bank was a test piece; it is dark green with embossed flowers. Marked "USA." $300.00 – 350.00.
The bank on the right was also a test piece, in an unusual light green glaze. Marked "8 27." $300.00 – 350.00.
The two test pieces were never put into productions. The dime banks hold $75.00 in dimes.

Plate 238: Standing Pig
Marked "© Hull USA 197." 8"h. $135.00 – 140.00.

Plate 239: Standing Pig
Color variation. $150.00 – 155.00.

Plate 240: Sitting Pig (Back and Front Views)
Marked "© Hull USA 196." $85.00 – 90.00.

Plate 241: Sitting Pig
Color variations. $120.00 – 130.00 each.

Plate 242: Corky (Back and Front Views)
Marked "Pat.Pend. Corky Pig © USA 1957." 5"h. $70.00 – 75.00.

Plate 243: Corky
Color variations. $70.00 – 75.00 each.

Plate 244: Corky
Color variations. $115.00 – 120.00 each.

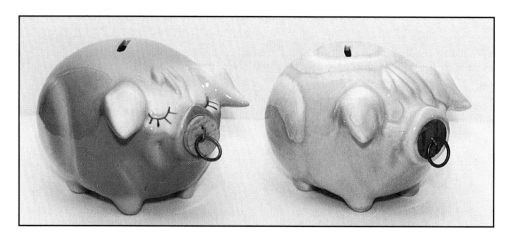

Plate 245: Corky
Color variations. $110.00 – 115.00 each.

Plate 246: Corky
Color variations. $110.00 – 115.00 each.

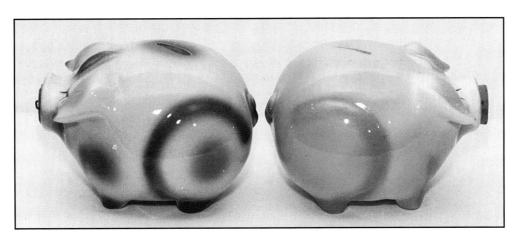

Plate 247: Corky
Color variations. $110.00 – 115.00 each.

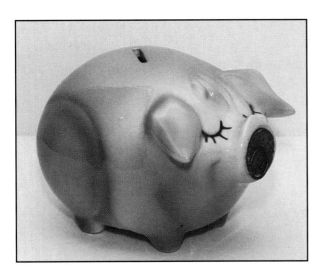

Plate 248: Corky
Color variation. $110.00 – 115.00.

Plate 249: Corky
Color variation, gold trim. $165.00 – 175.00.

Plate 250: Standing Pig with Embossed Flowers
Unmarked. 3½"h. $30.00 – 35.00.

Plate 251: Standing with Embossed Flowers
Marked "USA." 3¾"h. $30.00 – 35.00.

Graham Chevrolet, located at 1515 West 4th Street, Mansfield, Ohio, has a Little Texan painted on the front picture window of the building. Wes Jones, who began working at the dealership on July 1, 1939, and is still selling cars there, said that Jim Graham, the dealership owner, once lived in the Zanesville area, which is where the connection between Graham and Hull Pottery originated.

The Graham "Little Texan" bank was designed by Sam Marvicson, a former employee of the car dealer, from a photograph of Graham's son Bryan dressed in a cowboy outfit.

After the banks were made at the Hull plant, they were sent to the home of Gladys Showers of Crooksville, Ohio, to be decorated. Gladys originally handpainted samples of the banks in several color schemes and Jim Graham chose the colors for the Little Texan banks. We most often see the banks with a purple base, but a few were shipped with a tan base. The exact number produced is unknown. The banks were sometimes given away with the purchase of a new car and a number of them were also given to employees as Christmas gifts.

Submitted by Denny and Bev Huffman.

Plate 252: The Little Texan
Marked "© Graham 72." 9¾"h. $600.00 – 650.00.

JAPAN

The Disney banks made in Japan are shown in the Walt Disney section.

Plate 253: Sad Eye Joe (Padlock)
Marked "Knott's Berry Farm; Ghost Town, Calif." 6"h.
$55.00 – 60.00.

Plate 254: Spotted Dog (Padlock)
Marked "Japan." 6¾"h. $40.00 – 45.00.

Plate 255: Cat (Padlock)
Marked "Grantcrest Japan."
7"h. $40.00 – 45.00.

Plate 256: Dog (Padlock)
Marked "Grantcrest Japan." 7¼"h.
$40.00 – 45.00.

Plate 257: Deer (Padlock)
Unmarked. 7"h. $40.00 – 45.00.

Plate 258: Standing Pig (Padlock)
Paper label "Thames Hand Painted Japan."
7¼"h. $40.00 – 45.00.

Plate 259: Standing Pig Turn-about (Side View) (Padlock)
Paper label "Thames Hand Painted Japan." 8½"h. $50.00 – 55.00.

Plate 260: Standing Pig Turnabout
Side view.

Plate 261: Standing Pig Turnabout
Reverse side view.

Plate 262: Lying Pig (Padlock)
Printed on bank "For That Cadillac." Unmarked.
3½"h. $40.00 – 45.00.

Plate 263: Sitting Pig with Rhinestone Eyes
Unmarked. 5½"h. $40.00 – 45.00.

Plate 264: Kitten with Bow (Padlock)
Paper label "G Nov. Co. Japan." 6¼"h. $45.00 – 50.00.

Plate 265: Poodle (Padlock)
Unmarked. 6½"h. $45.00 – 50.00.

Plate 266: Pig Head (Padlock)
Marked "Thames Hand Painted Japan."
5½"h. $40.00 – 45.00.

Plate 267: Clown Head (Padlock)
Marked "Thames Hand Painted Japan Pat. Pend. Des."
6¼"h. $40.00 – 45.00.

Plate 268: Indian
Marked "Japan." 5¾"h. $40.00 – 45.00.

Plate 269: Indian Head
Marked "Japan." 4½"h.
$30.00 – 35.00.

Plate 270: Fi-Dough — To Make Both Ends Meet
Marked "Japan Created by Earl Bernard." 5"h. $30.00 – 35.00.

Plate 271: Puppy in a Basket
Marked "Japan." 6½"h. $20.00 – 25.00.

**Plate 272: Dog with Fur —
For Bills I Can't Forget**
Marked "Japan." 5¼"h. $25.00 – 30.00.

Plate 273: Sitting Dog
Marked "Japan." 6"h. $25.00 – 30.00.

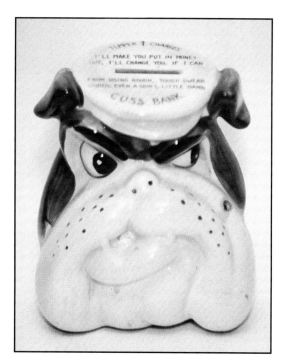

Plate 274: Dog Cuss Bank
Marked "3056." 5¼"h. $25.00 – 30.00.

Plate 275: Man Cuss Bank
Paper label "Japan." 5½"h. $25.00 – 30.00.

Plate 276: Clown Head
Marked "Japan." 6"h. $20.00 – 25.00.

Plate 277: Girl Head
Marked "Japan." 6¼"h. $30.00 – 35.00.

Plate 278: Indian (Nodder)
Marked "Japan."
5½"h. $40.00 – 45.00.

Plate 279: Chinese Nodder
Marked "Japan." 7"h. $40.00 – 45.00.

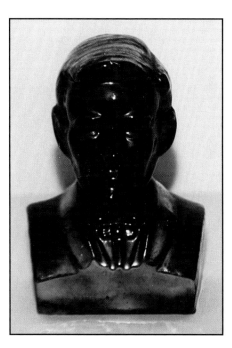

Plate 280: Abe Lincoln
Unmarked. 5"h. $25.00 – 30.00.

**Plate 281: Drunk —
Flings Aren't Free Save**
Marked "Davard Originals ©
Japan 1965." 7"h.
$25.00 – 30.00.

Plate 282: Indian Boy
With flasher eyes and rockers.
Marked "Japan." 5¾"h.
$30.00 – 35.00.

Plate 283: Monk
Marked "San Myro Japan." 5"h.
$15.00 – 18.00.

Plate 284: Before Taxes, After Taxes Turnabout (Side View)
Paper label "Made in Japan." 6¼"h.
$35.00 – 40.00.

Plate 285: Before Taxes, After Taxes Turnabout
"Before Taxes" side.

Plate 286: Before Taxes, After Taxes Turnabout
"After Taxes" side.

Plate 287: Mac Saver
Marked "From Helig Meyers Furniture Store Japan." 6¾"h. $20.00 – 25.00.

Plate 288: Girl with an Apple (Nodder)
Unmarked. 8¼"h. $60.00 – 65.00.

Plate 289: Boy On a Pig (Nodder)
Marked "Japan." 7"h.
$60.00 – 65.00.

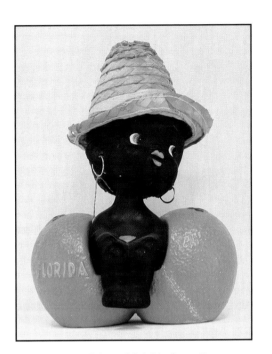

**Plate 290: Boy With
Watermelon (Nodder)**
Paper label "Made in Japan."
8½"h. $60.00 – 65.00.

**Plate 291: Girl Sitting On
Oranges (Nodder)**
Paper label "Kenmae Japan."
8"h. $60.00 – 65.00.

**Plate 292: Girl Sitting On
Watermelon (Nodder)**
Paper label "Made In Japan."
5½"h. $60.00 – 65.00.

**Plate 293: Girl With
Watermelon (Nodder)**
Unmarked. 7"h. $60.00 – 65.00.

Plate 294: Old King Cole
Marked "Japan." 5¼"h. $55.00 – 60.00.

Plate 295: Humpty Dumpty
Unmarked. 5"h. $75.00 – $80.00.

Plate 296: Humpty Dumpty on a Wall
Marked "Japan 3232." 6¼"h.
$65.00 – 70.00.

Plate 297: Pigs On a Trunk
Marked "Original Dee Bee Co. Imports;
Hand Painted Japan." 6"h. $60.00 - 65.00.

Plate 298: Standing Pig
Hand decorated flowers. Marked
"Japan." 3"h. $20.00 – 22.00.

Plate 299: Girl Pig
Paper label "Japan." 5½"h.
$35.00 – 40.00.

Plate 300: Boy Pig
Paper label "Japan." 5½"h.
$35.00 – 40.00.

Plate 301: Lazy Pig
Marked "Japan SYC." 6"h. $25.00 – 30.00.

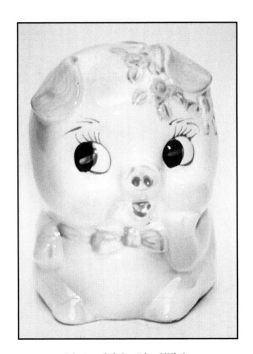

**Plate 302: Pig With
Embossed Flowers**
Unmarked. 6"h. $18.00 – 20.00.

Plate 303: Sitting Pig
Marked "Japan." 4¾"h. $22.00 – 25.00.

Plate 304: Standing Pig With Hat
Unmarked. 6"h. $25.00 – 28.00.

Plate 305: Monkey
Unmarked. 6¼"h. $22.00 – 25.00.

Plate 306: Smokey Bear
Marked "Japan." 3½"h.
$30.00 – 35.00.

Plate 307: Sitting Bear
Marked "Japan." 7"h. $15.00 – 18.00.

**Plate 308: Smokey Bear
With Gold Trim**
Paper label "West Pac Japan Hand Painted."
7"h. $100.00 – 110.00.

Plate 309: Deer and Fawn
Marked "T1864." 8"h. $35.00 – 40.00.

Plate 310: Owl
Marked "Japan." 5¼"h.
$20.00 – 22.00.

Plate 311: Owl
Marked "Japan China."
4½"h. $22.00 – 24.00.

Plate 312: Duck
Marked "Japan." 4¼"h. $25.00 – 30.00.

Plate 313: Squirrel
Paper label "Made In Japan." 4¾"h.
Tongue moves when coin is
dropped in. $45.00 – 50.00.

Plate 314: Cat With Hat
Marked "Made In Japan." 5"h. $25.00 – 30.00.

Plate 315: Deer In Rocking Chair
Paper label "Japan." 5¼"h.
Flasher eyes. $35.00 – 40.00.

**Plate 316: Rabbit In
Rocking Chair**
Paper label "Japan." 5¼"h. Flasher eyes.
$35.00 – 40.00.

Plate 317: Cat With Bow
Marked "Japan." 5½"h.
$20.00 – 24.00.

Plate 318: Telephone
Paper label "Japan." 9½"h.
$30.00 – 35.00.

Plate 319: For My Trip
Marked "Japan." 6½"h. $25.00 – 28.00.

Plate 320: Pot With Lid
Marked "Executive House Fine China Japan."
3¼"h. $10.00 – 12.00.

Plate 321: Cookies
Marked "Wyatt, Dunagan Williams, Inc.; 1901
Avenue of the Stars Los, Angeles, Calif;
Made In Japan." 5¼"h. $35.00 – 40.00.

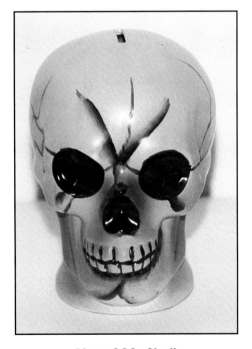

Plate 322: Skull
Paper label "ANCO Made in Japan." 5¼"h.
$18.00 – 20.00.

Plate 323: Li'l Devil
Marked "Japan." 7"h. $18.00 – 20.00.

**Plate 324: Santa Nodder
(Two Pieces)**
Marked "Sonsco Japan pat. E.K."
7¼"h. $50.00 – 55.00.

Plate 325: Santa On House
Marked "Japan for Spencer." 6"h.
$30.00 – 35.00.

Plate 326: Santa's Post Office
Paper label "Made in Japan."
6¾"h. $30.00 – 35.00.

Plate 327: Christmas Tree
Unmarked. 8¼"h. $30.00 – 35.00.

Plate 328: Snowman
Paper label "ARDCO Fine Quality
Made In Japan VX-201."
5"h. $30.00 – 35.00.

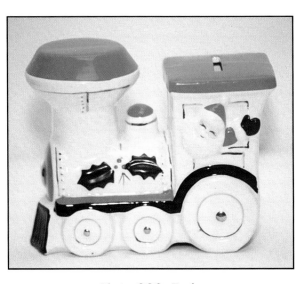

Plate 329: Train
Marked "International Product; Made in Japan."
5"h. $35.00 – 40.00.

Plate 330: Train
Reverse view.

Pottery By J.D. is located in Buckeye Lake, Ohio, owned and operated by J.D. James and his wife Pat. Pottery By J.D. is best known for its cookie jars which are designed by J.D. and hand decorated by Pat. The Peek-A-Boo bank was produced upon our request (as Regal China never made a bank to go with the cookie jar and shakers) and certainly did not fall short of our expectations. It's a favorite in our collection; the design, quality and workmanship are nothing short of fantastic.

Plate 331: Peek-A-Boo
Marked "Peek-A-Boo. Pottery by J.D."
10½"h. $150.00 – 175.00.

Plate 332: Peek-A-Boo
Side view.

Plate 333: Peek-A-Boo
Bottom view.

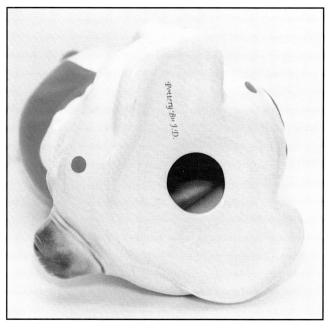

Plate 334: Waving Santa
Unmarked. 6¼"h. $25.00 – 30.00.

Plate 335: Waving Santa
Unmarked. 6"h. $25.00 – 30.00.

**Plate 336: Skunk Dresser
Caddy & Bank**
Marked "Kreiss & Co." 7¼"h.
$45.00 – 50.00.

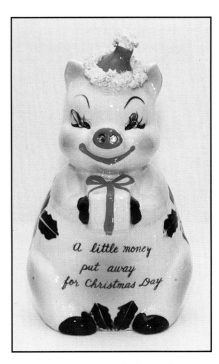

Plate 337: Standing Pig
4"h. $75.00 – 80.00.

Plate 338: Sitting Pig
6¾"h. $75.00 – 80.00.

Plate 339: Lying Pig
4"h. $75.00 – 80.00.

LEFTON CHINA COMPANY

George Zoltan Lefton Company began in 1940 as a Chicago based importer/distributor. Most Lefton pieces have a paper label and are marked "Made in Japan," and stamped with a number.

Plate 340: Hurbert Lion
Paper label, "Trade Mark Exclusive Japan Stamp - 413384." 7½"h.
$110.00 – 125.00.

Plate 341: Chick
Paper label "Lefton Japan." 5¾"h.
$40.00 – 45.00.

Plate 342: Birds On a Birdhouse
Unmarked. 5¾"h. $60.00 – 65.00.

Plate 343: Wishing Well
Paper label "Lefton Japan."
6¾"h. $50.00 – 55.00.

Plate 344: Frog
Paper label "Leftons Exclusive Japan." 4"h.
$35.00 – 40.00.

Plate 345: Mouse
Stamp "74302."
5¾"h. $35.00 – 40.00.

Plate 346: Owl (Padlock)
Stamp "1167."
5¾"h. $90.00 – 95.00.

Plate 347: Astronaut — For My Trip to the Moon
Paper label "Leftons Exclusive Japan."
8"h. $90.00 – 95.00.

LePere Pottery began its operation in 1936 on Glenwood Avenue in Zanesville, Ohio. LePere is best known for its copper luster ware. Much of LePere pottery is hand decorated, and many pieces are trimmed with gold.

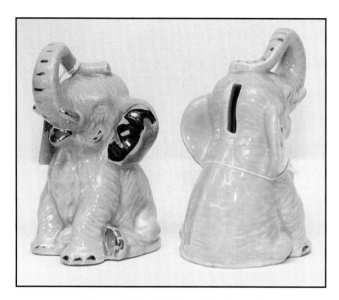

Plate 348: Sitting Elephant
Unmarked. Two color variations, gold trimmed.
5"h. $40.00 – 45.00 each.

Plate 349: Sitting Elephant
Unmarked. Color variations, cold paint.
5"h. $25.00 – 30.00 each.

Plate 350: Hound Dog
Unmarked. 4¾"h. Gold trimmed, $40.00 – 45.00.
No trim, $20.00 – 25.00.

Plate 351: Puppy
Unmarked. 5"h. Back and front views.
Gold trimmed. $40.00 – 45.00 each.

Plate 352: Standing Pig
Unmarked. Gold trimmed with decals.
2½"h x 6"l. $40.00 – 45.00 each.

Plate 353: Puppy
Color variations, gold trimmed. $40.00 – 45.00.

Plate 354: Standing Pig
Marked "The Home Shoppe Salineville, Ohio."
3½"h x 5½"l. Mold variation. Gold trimmed. $55.00 – 60.00.

Plate 355: Standing Pig
Mold variation. Unmarked. 4"h x 6½"l.
Gold trimmed. $100.00 – 110.00.

Plate 356: Standing Pig
Unmarked. 2½"h x 6"l. No trim, $20.00 – 25.00. Gold trim, $40.00 – 45.00.

Plate 357: Standing Pig
Color variations. Gold trim. $40.00 – 45.00 each.

Plate 358: Standing Pig
Color variations with gold trim. $40.00 – 45.00 each.

Plate 359: Sitting Pig
Color variations. 4½"h. No trim, $20.00 – 25.00. Gold trim, $40.00 – 45.00.

Plate 360: Sitting Pig
Mold variation, indented belly button. Unmarked. 4½"h. $40.00 – 45.00.

Plate 361: Sitting Pig
Back and bottom views.

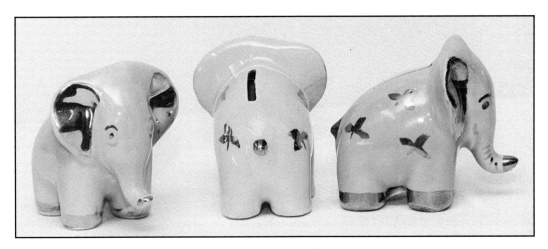

Plate 362: Standing Elephant
Unmarked. Gold trim. 3½"h. $40.00 – 45.00 each.

Plate 363: Football
Unmarked. Gold trim. 4"h x 5"l. $75.00 – 80.00.

Plate 364: Owl
Unmarked.
Gold trim.
8"h. $75.00 – 80.00.

Plate 365: Kitten
Unmarked. Cold paint. 4½"h. $25.00 – 30.00 each.

Plate 366: Kitten
Unmarked. Mold variation. $35.00 – 40.00.

Plate 367: Kitten
Color variation. Gold trim.
$40.00 – 45.00.

Plate 368: Kitten
Color variations.

Plate 369: Kitten
Color variation. Gold trim.
$40.00 – 45.00 each.

Plate 370: Kitten
Additional color variations.

Louisville Stoneware Co.

The Lousiville Stoneware Company began operation in 1906 and is located in Louisville, Kentucky. Their pieces are unique because they are made of stoneware.

Plate 371: Hot Air Balloon
Marked stamp "Louisville
Stoneware Made in Kentucky."
7½"h. $55.00 – 60.00.

Maddux of California

Maddux of California started in Los Angeles, California, in 1938. Their last year of manufacturing was 1974. After 1974 it became strictly a selling company.

Plate 373: Bear
Marked "Maddux
2311." 9¼"h.
$65.00 – 70.00.

Plate 372: Running Puppy
Marked "Maddux USA." 5¼"h. $75.00 – 80.00.

Plate 374: Bird
Marked "Maddux of Calif. USA."
9½"h. $40.00 – 45.00.

Plate 375: Owl
Marked "Maddux Calif. 3303." 10"h.
$40.00 – 45.00.

Plate 376: Pig
Paper label, "Manufactured by Maddux of California USA."
4¾"h. $50.00 – 55.00.

McCoy Pottery originated in 1848 in Zanesville, Ohio. In 1911, following a merger with George Brush of The Brush Pottery Company, the J.W. McCoy Pottery became the Brush-McCoy Pottery Company. Just prior to the merger, James W. McCoy and his son, Nelson, founded the McCoy Sanitary Stoneware Company in Roseville, Ohio. The McCoy interest in the Brush-McCoy Company was sold and the McCoy Sanitary Stoneware Company was expanded. The name was changed to the Nelson McCoy Company in 1922. The company continued to remain in the rein of the McCoy family until 1981. The company was then sold three times, the final time to Designer Accents of New Jersey in 1985. The doors were closed in December 1990. In the fall 1991, fire claimed the office portion of the former company.

Plate 377: Santa Head
Cookie jar/bank. Marked "McCoy Limited Design Nelson McCoy Limited Edition." 10¾"h. $295.00 – 325.00.

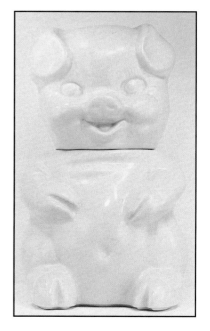

Plate 378: Bubbles
Cookie jar/bank. Marked "224 USA Lancaster McCoy." 9⅝"h. $175.00 – 200.00.

Plate 379: Cookie Bank
Cookie jar/bank. Marked "McCoy USA." 6½"h. $140.00 – 150.00.

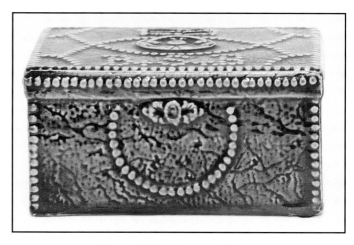

Plate 380: Money Chest
Marked "Replica, First Money Chest, 1834 Bowery Savings Bank." 3"h x 6"l. $65.00 – 70.00.

Plate 381: Seaman
Marked on cork bottom "The Seamans Bank & Savings." 5½"h. $60.00 – 65.00.

Plate 382: Kittens On a Barrel
Marked "USA." 6¼"h. $25.00 – 30.00.

Plate 383: Standing Pig
Marked "McCoy." 4¼"h. $40.00 – 45.00.

Plate 384: Standing Pig
Color variation.

Plate 385: Thrifty Tom Save For That Rainy Day
Marked "Where Thousands Save Millions; Whitestone Savings and Loan Association." 5½"h. $30.00 – 35.00

Plate 386: Mailbox
Unmarked. 4¾"h. $30.00 – 35.00.

Plate 387: Dime Bank and Dresser Caddy
Marked "D.S.B." 4¼"h. $45.00 – 50.00.

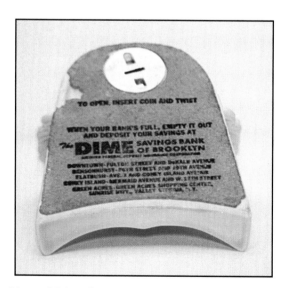

Plate 388: Dime Bank and Dresser Caddy
Bottom view.

Plate 389: Dollar Federal Barrel
Unmarked. 7"h. $20.00 – 25.00.

Plate 390: Metz Beer Barrel
Unmarked. 6¼"h. $20.00 – 25.00.

Plate 391: John Howard Statue
Marked "Howard Savings Institution,"
Chartered 1857 New Jersey." 9"h.
$25.00 – 30.00.

Plate 392: Mile Marker
Marked "Cumberland 208; Wheeling 78; Zanesville 4;
Columbus 49." 8"h. $35.00 – 40.00.

Plate 393: Clock Tower
Marked "General Office Tower;
Tower of Strength; The Williamsburg
Savings Bank." 7¼"h. $25.00 – 30.00.

Plate 394: Clock Tower
Color variation.

Plate 395: Rabbit
Marked "McCoy 1005." 10"h.
$75.00 – 80.00.

Plate 396: Clown
Marked "McCoy 1002." 9¾"h.
$75.00 – 80.00.

Plate 397: Building with Steeple
Marked "USA." 6¾"h. $25.00 – 30.00.

Plate 398: Smiley Face
Marked "USA." Large, 6½"h. $18.00 – 20.00.
Small, 4¾"h. $15.00 – 18.00.

Plate 399: Eagle – Wings Up
Marked "National Bank of Dayton."
7¾"h. $45.00 – 50.00.

Plate 400: Eagle – Wings Down
Marked "Industrial Saving Bank."
6¾"h. $30.00 – 35.00.

Plate 401: Cat On A Coal Bucket
Marked "McCoy LCC 219 USA." 9¾"h. $225.00 – 250.00.

Plate 402: Woodsy Owl
Marked, "®." 8½"h. Gold trim.
$110.00 – 125.00.

Plate 403: Hound Bank/Dresser Caddy
Unmarked. 6½"h. $35.00 – 40.00.

Plate 404: Lucky Penny Puppy
Unmarked. 6¾"h. $15.00 – 20.00.

Plate 405: Ghost – My Ghostly Savings
Unmarked. 8"h. $25.00 – 30.00.

Plate 406: Ghost – Who You Gonna Call
Unmarked. 7½"h. $25.00 – 30.00.

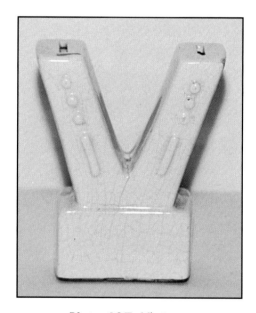

Plate 407: Victory
Unmarked. 5½"h. $140.00 – 150.00.

The miscellaneous section represents banks that have distinctive marks or labels but about which no other information is known.

Plate 408: Jalopy
Marked "Australia." 3½"h. $12.00 – 15.00.

Plate 409: Avon Bear
Unmarked. 6"h. $18.00 – 20.00.

Plate 410: Turtle
Paper label, "Collectable Editions Brinns 1987."
5"h. $25.00 – 28.00.

Plate 411: Football
Marked "WC Bunting, Wellsville, Ohio."
5½"h. $30.00 – 35.00.

Plate 412: Rabbit
Marked "Made in California."
$22.00 – 25.00.

Plate 413: Clown
Paper label "China."
4½"h. $18.00 – 22.00.

Plate 414: Dolly Dingle
Marked "Billy Bump, ™ Dolly Dingle Series ©
House of Global Art 1982." 4¾"h. $55.00 – 60.00.

Plate 415: Christmas Santa, Bear, and Snowman
All marked "Made in China." 5½"h. $22.00 – 24.00 each.

Plate 416: Chick With Hat
Marked "Ceramica Costa Rica."
9"h. $22.00 – 26.00.

Plate 417: Boy With Bow Tie
Marked "Duncan Ceramic Productions, Inc.
1970." 6"h. $24.00 – 26.00.

Plate 418: Paddington Bear Block
Marked "Colports – Made In England
Paddington & Co. Limited." 3¼"h.
$30.00 – 35.00.

Plate 419: Tennis Bear
Paper label, "Farrah International."
5¾"h. $22.00 – 24.00.

Plate 420: Pig In A Purse
Marked "Made in Germany, Souvenir of Columbus, O."
4"h. $28.00 – 30.00.

Plate 421: Clown Head
Marked "Gibson Greeting Card, Inc."
7"h. $18.00 – 20.00.

Plate 422: Monkey
Marked "HA." 5¾"h. $18.00 – 20.00.

Plate 423: Dino and Pebbles
Marked "© Hanna-Barbera Prod., Inc."
6½"h. $60.00 – 65.00.

Plate 424: Jetsons
Paper label "© 1986 Hanna-Barbera Prod.,
Inc." 3"h. $140.00 – 150.00.

Plate 425: Cricket
Marked "Helen Hargar." 6½"h.
$55.00 – 60.00.

Plate 426: Troll
Marked "International Silver Company; ©
The Troll Company; Norfin is a Reg. ™ of
EFS Mkg." 10"h. $45.00 – 50.00.

Plate 427: Cat
Paper label "Italy." 8½"h. $30.00 –
35.00.

Plate 428: Lion
Marked "Italy." 8½"h. $30.00 – 35.00.

Plate 429: Hunting Dog
Marked "JASCO." 5¼"h.
$24.00 – 26.00.

Plate 430: Egg Mailman
Marked "The JASCO Good Egg
Collection." 5"h. $22.00 – 24.00.

Plate 431: Spinach Can
Unmarked. 5"h. $13.00 – 14.00.

Plate 432: Spinach Can
Marked "1975 by King Features Syn.
Inc." 4"h. $22.00 – 24.00.

Plate 433: Sitting On The World
Marked "1987 King Features Syndicate." On
back "Hagar." 6"h. $25.00 – 30.00.

Plate 434: Woodstock
Paper label "Woodstock Corp; © 1965,
1972 United Features Syndicate, Inc."
6"h. $30.00 – 35.00.

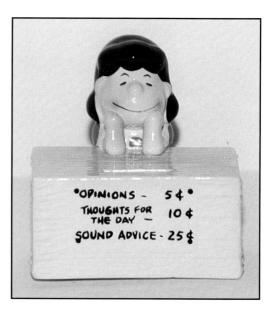

Plate 435: Lucy and Opinions Stand
Marked "© 1952, 1966 United Feature Syndicate, Inc. Willitts Designs." 4"h. $25.00 – 30.00.

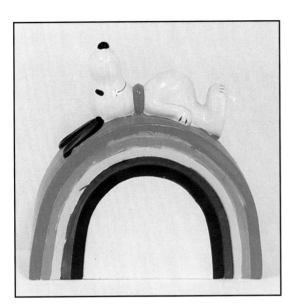

Plate 436: Snoopy On A Rainbow
Paper label "Made in Korea."
4¾"h. $25.00 – 30.00.

Plate 437: Nipper
Paper label "Nipper GE Comp. Made in Korea."
5¾"h. $25.00 – 30.00.

Plate 438: Dryer, Refrigerator, and Stove
Marked "©1987 Leadworks Inc." From 5¼"h. to 7"h. $50.00 – 55.00 each.

Plate 439: Tinman, Dorothy, Lion, and Scarecrow
All marked "© MGM 1989." 7"h. $85.00 – 90.00 each.

Plate 440: Tom and Jerry
Marked "© Metro Goldwyn Mayer Film Co.
1981." 5"h. $75.00 – 80.00.

Plate 441: Bear
Marked "Mid Ohio Marketing." 5"h. $35.00 – 40.00.

Plate 442: Artist Duck
Marked "Mexico." 9"h. $26.00 – 28.00.

Plate 443: Oscar
Marked "© Muppets, Inc." 6½"h.
$30.00 – 32.00.

Plate 444: Oscar With Pig
Marked "© Muppets Inc. 1970
Comp." 5¾"h. $30.00 – 32.00.

Plate 445: Cookie Monster
Marked "© Muppets Inc. 1976."
5¾"h. $30.00 – 32.00.

**Plate 446: Cookie
Monster With Cookie**
Marked "© Muppets, Inc."
5¾"h. $30.00 – 32.00.

Plate 447: Big Bird
Marked "Muppets, Inc. 1971 – 1978." 5½"h.
$30.00 – 32.00.

Plate 448: Ford Shaggy Dog
Says "Ford" on the collar, no other mark.
The Ford Shaggy Dog is a Don Winton
Design. 7½"h. $45.00 – 50.00.

Plate 449: Purse
Marked "Norcrest, crafted in Japan."
4½"h. $22.00 – 24.00.

Plate 450: Superman
Marked on back "Corr. 1949; Nat. Com.
Pub. Inc." 9½"h. $600.00 – 800.00.

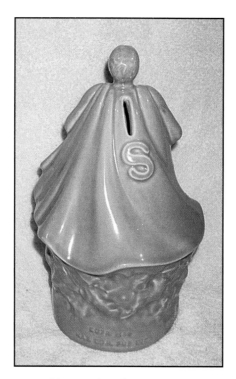

Plate 451: Superman
Back view.

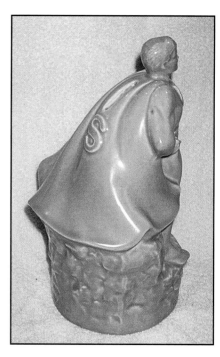

Plate 452: Superman
Side view.

Plate 453: Batman
Paper label "National Periodical
Publications Inc. 1966 Japan."
7"h. $125.00 – 130.00.

Plate 454: Robin
Paper label "National Periodical
Publications, Inc. 1966 Japan."
6½"h. $125.00 – 130.00.

**Plate 455: Pillsbury
Dough Boy**
Marked "© The Pillsbury Co."
7¼"h. $20.00 – 22.00.

Plate 456: Charlie Tuna
Marked "1988 Star Kist Foods,
Inc." 9½"h. $75.00 – 80.00.

Plate 457: Tom Cat
Marked "Tom Cat Takahashi San
Francisco Hand Painted." 6"h.
$45.00 – 50.00.

Plate 458: Grimace
Paper label "Grimace®; © 1985
McDonald's Corp. Thailand."
8½"h. $45.00 – 50.00.

Plate 459: Ronald McDonald
Unmarked. 7½"h. $60.00 – 65.00.

Plate 460: McDonald's Bag
Marked "Made exclusively for Group Communications Inc.; Hales Corners, 53130 in Thailand." 6¾"h. $45.00 – 50.00.

Plate 461: Heart Monkey
Marked "Playful Heart Monkey™ One of the Care Bear Cousins; American Greetings Corp. Cleveland, Ohio 44144." 5¾"h. $25.00 – 30.00.

Plate 462: Chef and Mammy
Paper label "Scotty; Made in Taiwan."
4"h. $20.00 – 22.00 each.

Plate 463: Mario
Paper label "Copyright ™ & ©1993; Nintendo All Rights Reserved Made in Taiwan." 11½"h. $25.00 – 30.00.

Plate 464: Yoshi
Marked same as Mario. 10¼"h.
$25.00 – 30.00.

Plate 465: Luigi
Marked same as Mario.
14"h. $25.00 – 30.00.

Plate 466: Bowser
Marked same as Mario. 10"h. $25.00 – 30.00.

Plate 467: Neal the Frog
Marked "Sears Roebuck & Co. 1977 Japan." 5"h.
$40.00 – 45.00.

Plate 468: C3P0
Marked "© Twentieth Century Fox Film
Corporation; U.S.A. Star Wars™." 7½"h.
Gold. $135.00 – 140.00.

Plate 469: R2D2
Marked same as C3P0. 8"h. $125.00 – 135.00.

Plate 470: Darth Vader
Marked same as C3P0. 7"h. $100.00 – 110.00.

Plate 471: Vulture
Marked "Quon-Quon
©MCMLXXX." 6½"h.
$30.00 – 32.00.

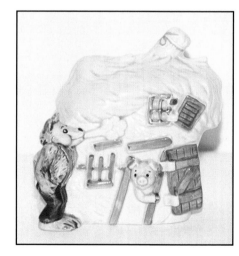

Plate 472: Three Little Pigs
Marked "Once Upon A Time ©1983
Quon-Quon; The Three Little Pigs Japan."
4½"h. $40.00 – 45.00.

The Morton Pottery Company began operation in Morton, Illinois, in 1922 and remained in the manufacturing business until 1976. Morton Pottery produced primarily utilitarian ware until the late 1930s at which time they introduced a novelty line.

Plate 473: Wall Hanging Pig – Feet Apart
No mark. 5¾"h. $60.00 – 65.00.

Plate 474: Wall Hanging Pig – Feet Together
No mark. 5¾"h. $60.00 – 65.00.

NATIONAL POTTERIES CORP.

The National Potteries Corp. (NAPCO), an import/distribution company, began operation in Cleveland, Ohio, in 1939. They relocated to Bedford, Ohio, and in 1984 moved to Jacksonville, Florida.

Plate 475: Boy Baby In Diaper
Marked "© NO 1960 JC4971." Paper label "National Potteries Co. Cleveland, OH; Made In Japan." 5¼"h. $65.00 – 70.00.

Plate 476: First Place Award
Paper label "NAPCO." 6¼" – 6½"h. $40.00 – 45.00 each.

Plate 477: Spaceship
Marked "NAPCO K5444." 6¼"h.
$200.00 – 210.00.

Plate 478: Rabbit
Marked "NAPCO Japan."
7"h. $25.00 – 30.00.

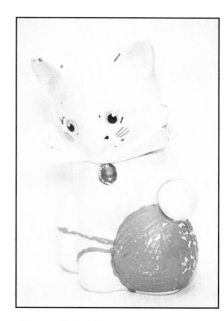

Plate 479: Kitten (Padlock)
Marked "NAPCO BOBBY."
6½"h. $40.00 – 45.00.

Plate 480: Hippo
Paper label "NAPCO."
5½"h. $25.00 – 30.00.

Plate 481: Fritz (Padlock)
Marked "Fritz ©NAPCO." 6¼"h. $40.00 – 45.00.

Plate 482: Billy (Padlock)
Marked "NAPCO Billy." 6"h. $40.00 – 45.00.

Plate 483: House With Pony (Padlock)
Marked "NAPCO Ceramic G2159." 5½"h. $30.00 – 32.00.

Plate 484: House With Cat (Padlock)
Marked "G2059." 6"h. $30.00 – 32.00.

Plate 485: Bear and Beehive
Marked "By NAPCO." 4¾"h. $25.00 – 30.00.

NOUVELLE POTTERY

Nouvelle Pottery was located in Zanesville, Ohio, from 1946 to the mid 1970s. Most Nouvelle Pottery was manufactured from customers' requests and made to their specifications. An example are Elmer and Elsie salt and pepper shakers made for Borden's Milk Company and marked "© Borden Co."

Plate 486: Cowboy
Marked "Nouvelle Pottery
Zanesville, Ohio." 7¾"h.
$75.00 – 80.00.

Plate 487: Cowboy
Color variation.

OTAGIRI

Imported from Japan.

Plate 488: Bird and Stump
Marked "© Otagiri 1980." 5½"h.
$25.00 – 30.00.

Plate 489: Covered Wagon
Marked "© D. Mayer Otagiri
Japan." 3½"h. $25.00 – 30.00.

The Omnibus Corporation (OCI) is owned by Fitz and Floyd of Dallas, Texas, which was established in 1960 and is currently in business today.

Plate 490: Bank Building
Marked "OCI 1982." 6½"h.
$28.00 - 30.00.

Plate 491: Milk Carton
Paper label "© OCI." 6¼"h.
$12.00 – 15.00.

J.B. Owens Pottery started in Roseville, Ohio, in 1885. In 1891 the company was moved to Zanesville, Ohio, specializing in stoneware. Art pottery was made between 1896 and 1907 at which time the Zanesville company was closed. Much of Owens Pottery is unmarked.

Plate 492: Pig
Unmarked. 2½"h. x 4"l. $135.00 – $145.00.

Plate 493: The Lucky Pig Bank
Unmarked. 3¼"h. x 5¼"l. $135.00 – 145.00.

An article from the *China, Glass and Pottery Review*, dated 1900 states: "The Lucky Pig Bank" is a novelty that the J.B. Owens Pottery Co. have recently put upon the market, and which has met with unusual success. The accompanying illustration shows this article, and as a department novelty it stands alone in this particular field. It sells for $4.50 a gross, and this admits of a retail price of five cents, which is a good profit to dealers. The firm have been kept very busy on these, but their facilities are such that they are in position to meet all demands. We would advise dealers to lay in a stock of these goods, as they will prove attractive to the Summer trade.'

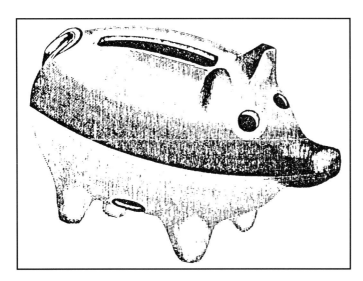

Plate 494: Lucky Pig Bank
Illustration from *China, Glass and Pottery Review*, May 1900.

Pearl China Co.

The Pearl China Company, known primarily as a selling company, had a direct connection with Pioneer Pottery Company from the mid 1930s to 1958 in East Liverpool, Ohio. It was not uncommon for a selling company to have control of or own a pottery company in order to expand its product line.

Plate 495: Rocking Horse
Marked "Pearl China Co. 22 K Gold." 5¼"h. $45.00 – 50.00.

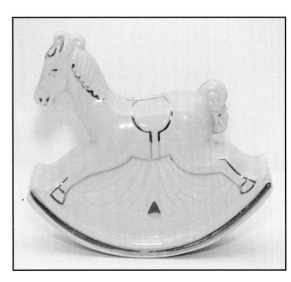

Plate 496: Rocking Horse
Color variation.

Plate 497: Squirrel
Marked "Pearl China Co. Hand Decorated
22 K Gold." 7¼"h. $75.00 – 80.00.

Plate 498: Standing Pig
Marked "Pearl China Co." 3"h. $28.00 – 30.00.

Plate 499: Small Standing Pig
Marked "Pearl China Co." 3¼"h. $22.00 – 24.00.

Plate 500: Bear
Marked "Pearl China Co. Hand Decorated 22 K
Gold USA." 7"h. $75.00 – 80.00.

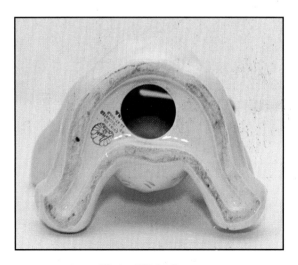

Plate 501: Bear
Bottom view.

Regal China was manufactured in Antioch, Illinois, from 1938 to 1992.

Plate 502: Monkey
Marked "C. Miller©." Cold paint. Bank slot
in top of hat. 11¼"h. $95.00 – 100.00.

Plate 503: Monkey (Bank/Lamp)
Marked "C. Miller ©." Cold paint. Bank slot
in pocket. 11¼"h. $200.00 – 225.00.

Plate 504: Monkey
Same as Plate 502, except underglaze
instead of cold paint. $125.00 – 130.00.

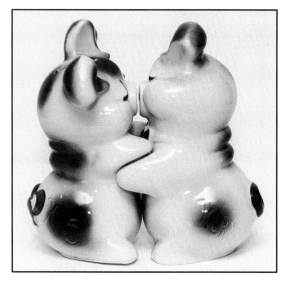

Plate 505: Bendel Pigs
Marked "Corp. 1958 R. Bendel Pat. No 2560755." "His"
is on the side of one pig. "Hers" is on the side of the
other pig. 6½"h. $650.00 – 700.00. The Bendel Pigs are
named after their designer, Ruth Van Tellingen Bendel.

Plate 506: Bendel Pigs
Front view.

Rosemeade Pottery was manufactured by Wahpeton Pottery Company in Wahpeton, North Dakota, from 1940 to 1961. The pottery was labeled with a Prairie Rose sticker and/or a stamp on the base. The North Dakota clay has a distinctive red color. Some pieces may be found where a white clay has been used; This was experimental clay shipped in from Kentucky. Add about 25% to the price on white clay pieces.

Plate 507: Buffalo
Marked "Rosemeade."
3½"h. $200.00 – 225.00.

The Roseville Pottery Company was located in Zanesville, Ohio, from 1892 to 1954.

Plate 508: Frog
Unmarked. 4¼"h.
$120.00 – 130.00.

Plate 509: Standing Pig
Unmarked. 2½"h. X 5"l. $100.00 – 125.00.

Plate 510: Standing Pig
Unmarked. 2½"h. X 5"l. $100.00 – 125.00.

Royal Copley

Spalding China Company of Sebring, Ohio, began in the 1930s making clock cases. In 1942 production of pottery artware began and continued through 1957. It is thought that pieces marked Royal Copley were marketed through one group of department stores and those marked Royal Windsor were marketed through another group of department stores. All were produced by the Spalding China Company.

Plate 511: Pig With Top Hat
Unmarked. 7½"h. Gold trim. $40.00 – 45.00.

Plate 512: Pig With A Wig
Unmarked. 6"h. $40.00 – 45.00.

Plate 513: Pig With A Wig
Color variation. $40.00 – 45.00.

Plate 514: Chicken Feed
Unmarked. 7½"h. $40.00 – 45.00.

Plate 515: Parky
Marked "FNB 1973." 7"h. $30.00 – 35.00 each.

Plate 516: Parky
Color variation. $30.00 – 35.00.

Plate 517: Pig With Bow Tie
Two color variations. Unmarked. $30.00 – 35.00 each.

Plate 518: Pig With Scarf
Unmarked. 5½"h. $30.00 – 35.00.

Plate 519: Bear
Unmarked. 7½"h. $40.00 – 45.00.

Royal Daulton

Plate 520: Bunnykins
Marked "Royal Daulton LTD 1936." $50.00 – 55.00.

**Plate 521: Mammy
With Hands On Hip**
Marked "Made by SaCorl."
5"h. $25.00 – 30.00.

Disney Banks distributed by Schmid can be found in the Walt Disney section.

Plate 522: Thomas
Marked "© Britt Allcraft Thomas Limited 1994." 3"h. $30.00 – 35.00.

The Shawnee Pottery Company was located in Zanesville, Ohio, from 1937 until 1961.

Plate 523: Tumbling Bear
Unmarked. 5"h. $175.00 – 200.00.

Plate 524: Bulldog
Unmarked. 4½"h. $175.00 – 200.00.

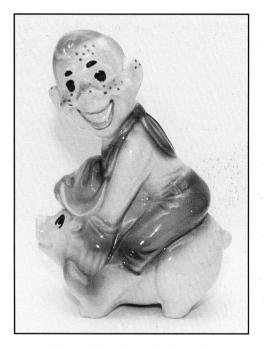

Plate 525: Howdy Doody
Marked "Bob Smith USA." 6¾"h. $500.00 – 550.00

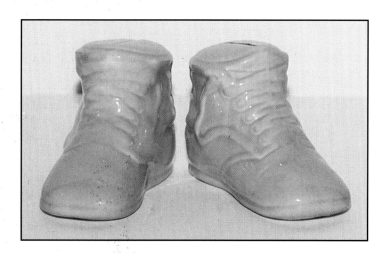

Plate 526: Shoes (Left and Right)
Unmarked. 3"h. $18.00 – 20.00.

The Howdy Doody Bank is said to have been produced in 1950 for approximately one year. Production was ceased due to copyright infringement.

Plate 527: Winnie Cookie Jar/Bank
Marked "Patented Winnie Shawnee 61 USA." 10½"h.
Butterscotch color, gold trim. $900.00 – 1,000.00.

Plate 528: Smiley Cookie Jar/Bank
Marked "Patented Smiley Shawnee 60 USA." 10½"h.
Butterscotch color, no gold. $550.00 – 575.00.

Plate 529: Winnie Cookie Jar/Bank
Marked "Patented Winnie Shawnee 61 USA." 10½"h.
Chocolate color, gold trim. $900.00 – 1,100.00.

Plate 530: Smiley Cookie Jar/Bank
Marked "Patented Smiley Shawnee 60 USA." 10½"h.
Chocolate color, gold trim. $850.00 – 875.00.

The new Shawnee Pottery, owned by Cecil Rapp, is currently in operation in Columbus, Ohio. The pottery is marked Shawnee on the bottom and has a Shawnee paper label. As yet, the new Shawnee Pottery Company has not reproduced any of the original Shawnee pieces. It is a quality pottery and all pieces are hand decorated. Dealers and collectors should educate themselves on what pieces were produced by the original Shawnee Pottery to avoid paying original Shawnee prices for a piece of the new.

Plate 531: Farmer Pig and Sowly
Marked "Shawnee Pottery 3/100." 5½"h. $75.00 for the pair.

Plate 532: Pekingese
Marked "Shawnee Pottery 4/250." 3½"h.

Plate 533: Deer
Marked "Shawnee Pottery 4/250." 4½"h.

Plate 534: Bear
Marked, "Shawnee Pottery 4/250." 4¾"h.

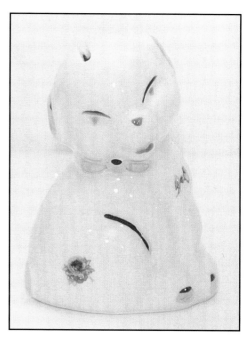

Plate 535: Puppy
Marked "Shawnee Pottery 4/250." 5"h.

The mark "Shawnee Pottery" is in raised letter. The 4/250 indicates that the banks are the fourth set of 250 sets produced.

Plate 536: Squirrel
Marked "Shawnee Pottery 4/250." 4½"h.

Plate 537: Rabbit
Marked "Shawnee Pottery 4/250." 4¼"h.

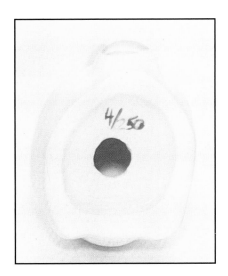

Plate 538: Rabbit
Bottom view. Marked
"Shawnee Pottery 4/250."

Plate 539: All Six Animal Banks
$200.00 for the set.

Sierra Vista was a family-owned company based in Pasadena, California, from 1944 through the 1950s. Starnes was a distributor named after Walter Starnes. We have included Starnes in this section because a major portion of Starnes pottery was made by Sierra Vista Ceramics.

Plate 540: Davy Crockett
Paper label "Handmade Starnes."
5¼"h. $400.00 – 450.00.

Plate 541: Squirrel
Paper label "Hand Painted Sierra Vista
Ceramics; Pasadena,
California." 5"h. $75.00 – 80.00.

Plate 542: Clown Head
Marked "USA." 5¾"h. $45.00 – 50.00.

Plate 543: Clown Head
Color variation. $45.00 – 50.00.

Plate 544: Rooster
Unmarked. 6"h. $50.00 – 55.00.

Plate 545: Jalopy
Unmarked. 4"h. $50.00 – 55.00.

Plate 546: Tug Boat
Unmarked. 4¼"h. $55.00 – 60.00.

Plate 547: Clown With Top Hat
Unmarked. 5"h. $30.00 – 35.00.

Plate 548: Chewbacca
Marked "Lucasfilm Ltd.; Designed
by Sigma the Tastesetter." 9¾"h.
$75.00 – 80.00.

Plate 549: Yoda
Marked "LFL; Designed by Sigma
the Tastesetter." 7½"h.
$90.00 – 95.00.

Plate 550: Jabba The Hut
Marked "Jabba The Hut; Return of the Jedi
designed by Sigma the Tastesetter."
7"h. $75.00 – 80.00.

Plate 551: Miss Piggy
Marked "© Sigma." 7¾"h.
$35.00 – 40.00.

**Plate 552: Thumper
on Block**
Paper label "Sigma Thumper."
6¼"h. $30.00 – 35.00.

Plate 553: Kliban Cat
Made of composition. Marked "Kliban Sigma."
4"h. x 6"l. $60.00 – 65.00.

Plate 554: Gardening Pig
Marked "Starset," paper label
"Star Creations." 6½"h.
$35.00 – 40.00.

Terrace Ceramics Inc. was located in Marietta and Zanesville, Ohio, from 1960 to January 1975. From 1960 to 1965 Terrace Ceramics was an exclusive distributor for American Pottery Company located in Marietta, Ohio. In 1964 the Terrace Ceramics offices were moved from Marietta to Zanesville, Ohio. John F. Bonistall, formerly from Shawnee Pottery, owned Terrace Ceramics and designed the ware, which was made by several different pottery companies. The first line marketed by Terrace Ceramics was manufactured by Haeger Potteries. McNichol China Company of Clarksburg, West Virginia, made a line of cookie jars for Terrace Ceramics to sell. Terrace Ceramics also marketed a line of corn ware. The corn line and several of the cookie jars are facsimiles of Shawnee Pottery as Bonistall purchased some of the Shawnee molds when the Shawnee Pottery Company went out of business.

Plate 555: Winnie Pig Cookie Jar/Bank
10¼"h. Marked "USA."
$350.00 – 375.00.

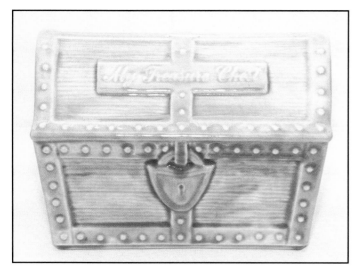

Plate 556: Treasure Chest
Marked "Terrace Ceramics." 9¾"l. x 6¼"h. $80.00 – 85.00.

Plate 557: Frog On A Log
Marked "2263 USA." (The frog is from a Brush Pottery mold.) 5½"h. $90.00 – 95.00.

Treasure Craft

Treasure Craft began operations in 1946 and is located in Compton, California. Don Winton of Twin Winton Pottery became associated with Treasure Craft in 1975 and still does some work for them. Pfaltzgraff acquired Treasure Craft in 1993. The Disney pieces that were manufactured by Treasure Craft are in the Walt Disney section.

Plate 558: Farmer Pig
Marked "Treasure Craft © Made in USA." 8½"h. $75.00 – 80.00.

Plate 559: Rocking Horse
Marked "Treasure Craft © Made in USA." 7"h. $70.00 – 75.00.

Plate 560: Hobo
Marked "Treasure Craft © USA."
8"h. $60.00 – 65.00.

Plate 561: Monk
Marked "Treasure Craft © USA."
7½"h. $30.00 – 35.00.

Plate 562: Ice Wagon
Marked "Treasure Craft © USA."
5½"h. $40.00 – 45.00.

Plate 563: Stagecoach
Marked "Treasure Craft © USA."
6½"h. $40.00 – 45.00.

Plate 564: Covered Wagon
Marked "Treasure Craft © USA."
5"h. $40.00 – 45.00.

Plate 565: Money Sack
Marked "Treasure Craft © USA."
6¾"h. $35.00 – 40.00.

Plate 566: Baseball Bunny
Marked "Treasure Craft 1961
Compton Calif." 6½"h.
$35.00 – 40.00.

Plate 567: Dog
Marked "Treasure Craft 1951 Compton
Calif." 8"h. $35.00 – 40.00.

Plate 568: Smiley
Marked "Treasure Craft © Made in
USA." 6"h. $65.00 – 70.00.

Plate 569: Famous Amos Cookie
Marked "Treasure Craft."
7"h. $65.00 – 70.00.

Twin Winton Pottery began in 1936. At the age of 16, Don Winton and his twin brother Ross began a business in partnership with Helen Burke, forming Burke-Winton. Don designed, his twin brother Ross was the moldman and business manager, and Helen Burke did the hand decorating and sales. In 1939 the Wintons went on their own. The brothers put the business on hold in 1943 to join the military, and resumed in 1946, at which time their brother Bruce joined them as their business manager. In 1952 Don and Ross sold their interest to Bruce and began freelancing. With the support of his wife Norma, Don continues to design.

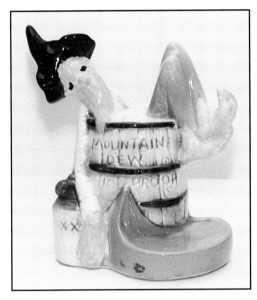

Plate 570: Hillbilly
Marked "Made in USA 38." 6¾"h. $125.00 –
150.00. (The Hillbilly Line began in 1947.)

Plate 571: Hillbilly
Back view.

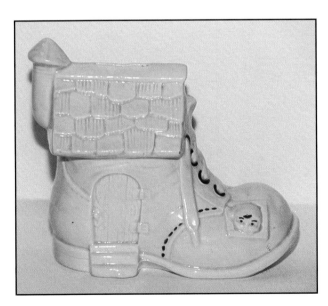

Plate 572: Child In Shoe
Unmarked. 6¾"h. $65.00 – 70.00.

Plate 573: Shack
Marked "Twin Winton © Calif. USA."
7"h. $50.00 – 55.00.

Plate 574: Friar
Marked "© Twin Winton Calif. USA." (Small) Dime Bank,
5½"h. $75.00 – 80.00. (Large), 8½"h. $35.00 – 40.00.

Plate 575: Friar
Color variation. Glossy dark brown
glaze. $50.00 – 55.00.

Plate 576: Rabbit
Marked "Twin Winton ©."
10"h. $60.00 – 65.00.

Plate 577: Squirrel
Marked "Twin Winton ©." 8"h.
$45.00 – 50.00.

Plate 578: Squirrel
Color variation. $60.00 – 65.00.

Plate 579: Cop
Marked "Twin Winton Calif. USA."
9"h. $50.00 – 55.00.

Plate 580: Cop
Color variation. $65.00 – 70.00.

Plate 581: Elephant
Marked "Twin Winton ©." 7¾"h.
$60.00 – 65.00.

Plate 582: Ranger Bear
Marked "Twin Winton." 8"h.
$50.00 – 55.00.

Plate 583: Lamb
Unmarked. 8¼"h. $50.00 – 55.00.

Plate 584: Teddy Bear
Marked "Twin Winton © Calif. USA 409."
7¼"h. $60.00 – 65.00.

Plate 585: Pig
Marked "Twin Winton."
8½"h. $60.00 – 65.00.

Plate 586: Pig
Color variation.
$75.00 – 80.00.

Plate 587: Dutch Girl
Marked "Twin Winton © Calif. USA."
8½"h. $45.00 – 50.00.

Plate 588: Dobbin
Marked "© Twin Winton Calif. USA."
9"h. $75.00 – 80.00.

Plate 589: Hotei
Marked "Twin Winton Calif. USA."
8"h. $55.00 – 60.00.

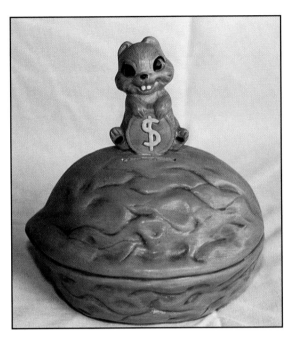

Plate 590: Nut
Marked "Twin Winton Calif. USA."
7¾"h. $55.00 – 60.00.

Plate 591: Poodle
Marked "Twin Winton USA."
9"h. $65.00 – 70.00.

Plate 592: Elf
Marked "Twin Winton Calif. USA."
8½"h. $65.00 – 70.00.

Plate 593: Pirate Fox
Marked "Twin Winton Calif. USA."
8½"h. $75.00 – 80.00.

This section contains numerous banks that are desired by collectors. They are in this section because we have not been able to find any information to enable us to positively identify them. Unlike the miscellaneous section, the banks in this section have no identifying marks on them. Most of them probably had paper labels that have been removed. We welcome any information you may have on these banks to be included in future editions and updates.

Plate 594: Flintstones
Unmarked. 7–7¼"h. $200.00 set.

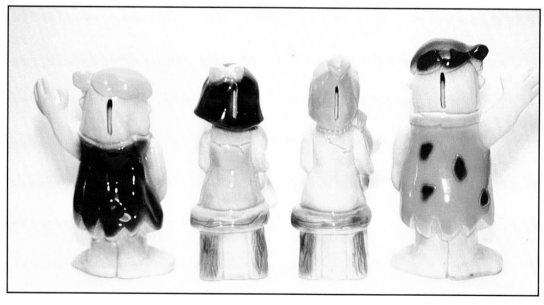

Plate 595: Flintstones
Back view.

Plate 596: Black Woman
Unmarked. 6½"h.
$25.00 – 28.00.

**Plate 597: Black
Woman**
Color variation.

Plate 598: Soldier (Nodder)
Unmarked. 9¼"h. $45.00 – 50.00.

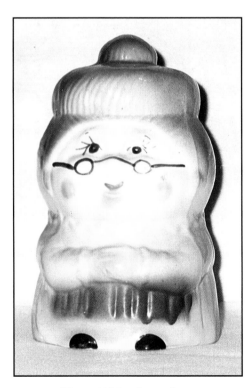

Plate 599: Grandma
Unmarked. 10"h. $22.00 – 25.00.

Plate 600: Uncle Sam
Unmarked. 6¾"h. $20.00 – 22.00.

Plate 601: Indian and TP
Unmarked. 5¾"h. $20.00 – 22.00.

Plate 602: Outhouse
Unmarked. 5¾"h. $18.00 – 20.00.

Plate 603: Sitting Pig
Unmarked. 4½"h. $20.00 – 22.00.

Plate 604: Sitting Pig
Side view.

Plate 605: Pig
Two color variations. Unmarked. 4¼"h. $18.00 – 20.00 each.

Plate 606: Pig
Mold variation. Unmarked.
4½"h. $18.00 – 20.00.

Plate 607: Pig
Unmarked. 2¾"h. $20.00 – 22.00.

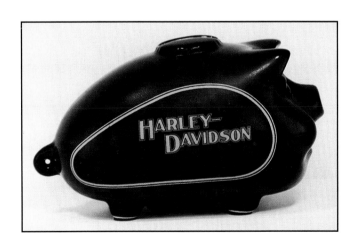

Plate 608: Harley Davidson Gas Tank
Unmarked. 3½"h. $45.00 – 50.00.

Plate 609: Harley Davidson Gas Tank
Unmarked. 7"h. $85.00 – 90.00.

Plate 610: Harley Davidson Gas Tank
Marked "Reproduction of 1935 model year Gas Tank Design." 7¼"h. $125.00 – 150.00.

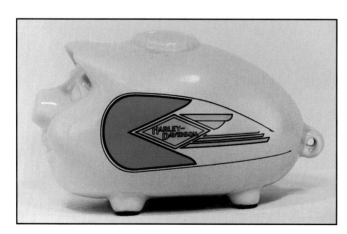

Plate 611: Harley Davidson Gas Tank
Unmarked. 3½"h. $65.00 – 70.00.

Plate 612: Harley Davidson Gas Tank
Marked "© 1933 H.D." 4"h. $40.00 – 45.00.

Plate 613: Jalopy
Unmarked. 4"h. $35.00 – 40.00.

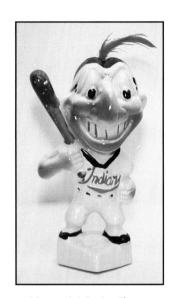

**Plate 614: Indians
Baseball Player**
Unmarked. 7"h. $250.00 – 275.00.

**Plate 615: Indians Baseball
Player With Baseball**
Marked "© CBC-Gibbs-Conner & Co."
6½"h. $300.00 – 325.00.

Plate 616: Cardinal
Unmarked. 7½"h. $250.00 – 275.00.

Plate 617: Baseball Cap
Unmarked. 3"h. $18.00 – 20.00.

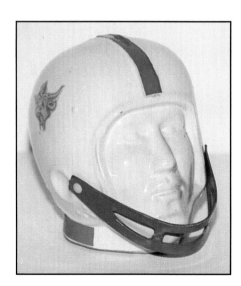

Plate 618: Football Player Head
Marked "Robert B. Vance & Assoc.©."
5"h. $23.00 – 25.00.

Plate 619: Football Helmet
Unmarked. 4½"h. $23.00 – 25.00.

Plate 620: Confederate Hat
Unmarked. 2¾"h. $18.00 – 20.00.

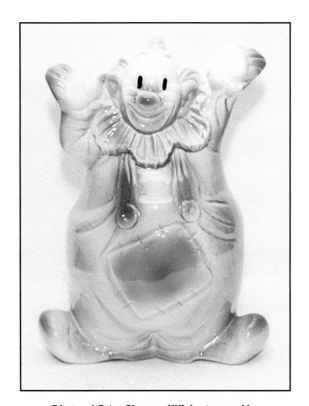

Plate 621: Clown With Arms Up
Unmarked. 11"h. $75.00 – 80.00.

Plate 622: Clown With Patches
Unmarked. 5½"h. $20.00 – 22.00.

Plate 623: Clown Head
Unmarked. 6"h. $25.00 – 30.00.

**Plate 624: Clown
With Umbrella**
Unmarked. 6¾"h. $25.00 – 30.00.

Plate 625: Clown On Base
Unmarked. 10"h. $65.00 – 70.00.

Plate 626: Hershey Chef
Unmarked. 6"h. $65.00 – 70.00.

Plate 627: Hershey Chef
Back view.

Plate 628: Olive Oyl
Unmarked. 11¼"h.
$60.00 – 65.00.

Plate 629: Tooth Fairy
Unmarked. 8¼"h. $20.00 – 22.00.

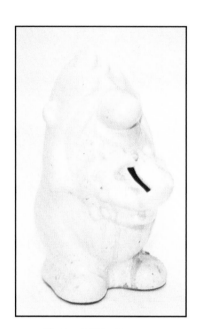

Plate 630: Beggar
Unmarked. 6¼"h.
$18.00 – 20.00.

Plate 631: Monk
Unmarked. 6¾"h. $25.00 – 30.00.

Plate 632: Monk
Unmarked. 7¼"h. $25.00 – 30.00.

**Plate 633: Uncle Sam
On Money Sack**
Unmarked. 8¼"h. $25.00 – 30.00.

Plate 634: Hillbilly
Unmarked. 7½"h. $20.00 – 22.00.

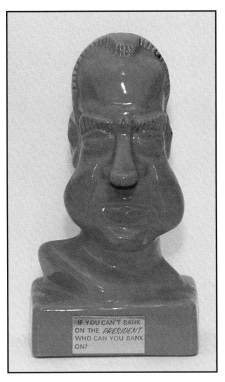

Plate 635: Nixon
Unmarked. 8½"h. $25.00 – $28.00.

Plate 636: Jetsons (Composition)
Unmarked. 5"H. $125.00 – $130.00.

Plate 637: Hobo
Marked "Thoman." 8¾"h.
$75.00 – $80.00.

Plate 638: Hobo
Marked "Thoman." 11"h. $75.00 – $80.00.

Plate 639: Train With Conductor
Unmarked. 4½"h. $25.00 – 28.00.

**Plate 640:
Entenmann's Chef**
Unmarked. 10"h. $45.00 – 50.00.

Plate 641: Smurf
Unmarked. 10"h.
$20.00 – 22.00.

**Plate 642:
Astronaut**
Unmarked. 4¾"h.
$22.00 – 24.00.

**Plate 643:
Smiley Face**
Unmarked. 4½"h.
$22.00 – $24.00.

Plate 644: Smiley Girl and Smiley Boy
Marked "Bryron Mold 1971." 6½"h. $18.00 – 20.00 each.

Plate 645: ET
Marked "634 and 650."
9¼"h. $25.00 – 30.00.

Plate 646: ET
Unmarked. 6"h. $25.00 – 30.00.

**Plate 647: California
Raisin With Sax**
Unmarked. 6½"h. $25.00 – 30.00.

**Plate 648: California Raisin
With Microphone**
Unmarked. 7"h. $25.00 – 30.00.

Plate 649: Dog
Unmarked. 7"h. $30.00 – 35.00.

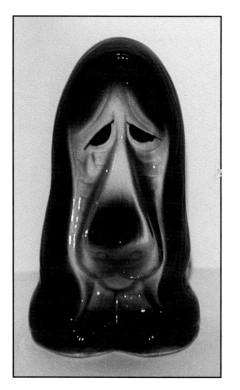

Plate 650: Hound Dog
Unmarked. 9½"h. $20.00 – 25.00.

Plate 651: Paddy
Unmarked. 6"h. $20.00 – 25.00.

Plate 652: Sheriff Dog
Unmarked. 6½"h. 18.00 – $20.00.

Plate 653: Tennis Mouse
Marked "Made In Italy."
7½"h. $18.00 – 20.00.

Plate 654: Bear on Base
Unmarked. 8½"h. $65.00 – 70.00.

**Plate 655: Smokey The Bear With Shovel
Smokey The Bear With Bucket**
Unmarked. 6¼"h. $125.00 – 135.00 each.

**Plate 656: Standing
Smokey The Bear**
Marked "A-478." 8"h. $165.00 – 170.00.

Plate 657: Bear
Unmarked. 5¼"h.
$15.00 – 18.00.

Plate 658: Lion
Unmarked. 6¾"h.
$18.00 – 20.00.

Plate 659: Lamb
Unmarked. 11"h. $25.00 – 28.00.

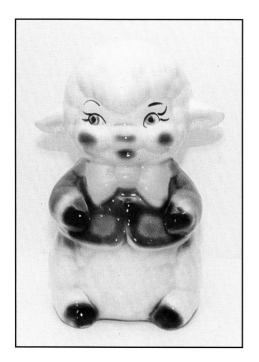

Plate 660: Lamb
Color variation.

Plate 661: Monkey On Base
Unmarked. 8½"h. $65.00 – 70.00.

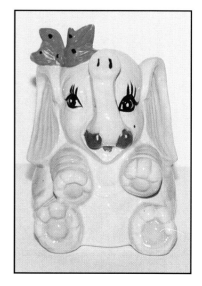

Plate 662: Elephant With Bow
Unmarked. 6"h. $18.00 – 20.00.

Plate 663: Standing Elephant
Unmarked. 6¾"h. $20.00 – 22.00.

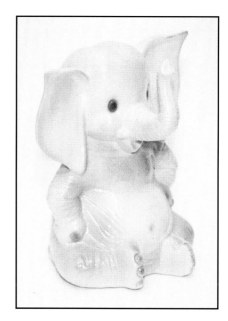

Plate 664: Sitting Elephant
Unmarked. 6½"h. $22.00 – 24.00.

Plate 665: I Love Atlantic City Elephant
Unmarked. 5¾"h. $18.00 – 20.00.

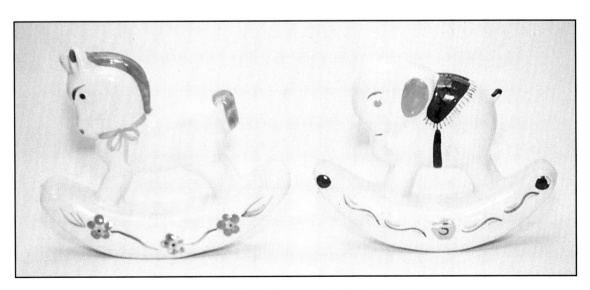

Plate 666: Sitting Elephant
Unmarked. 6½"h. $15.00 – 18.00.

Plate 667: Lying Elephant
Unmarked. 4¼"h. $15.00 – 18.00.

Plate 668: Rocking Horse and Rocking Elephant
Unmarked. 4½"h. $22.00 – 24.00.

Plate 669: Standing Elephant
Unmarked. 4¼"h.
$18.00 – 20.00.

**Plate 670: Skunk
Bank/Dresser Caddy**
Unmarked. 6¼"h. $35.00 – 40.00.

Plate 671: Skunk
Unmarked. 5¼"h.
$20.00 – 25.00.

Plate 672: Give A Hoot Owl
Unmarked. 7½"h. $22.00 – 24.00.
Reproduction of McCoy Woodsey Owl.

Plate 673: Owl
Unmarked. 5½"h.
$18.00 – 20.00.

Plate 674: Owl
Unmarked. Pottery bottom screws on.
6½"h. $25.00 – 28.00.

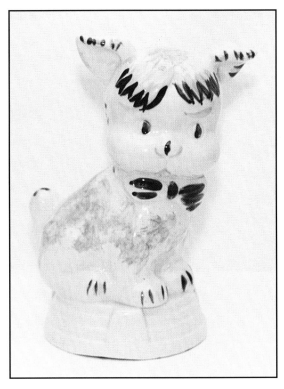

Plate 675: Dog On A Base
Unmarked. 8½"h. $65.00 – 70.00.

Plate 676: Kitty In Airplane
Unmarked. 8"h. $25.00 – 30.00.

Plate 677: Cat With A Bow
Unmarked. 7"h. $25.00 – 30.00.

Plate 678: Persian Cat
Unmarked. 5½"h. $18.00 – 20.00.

Plate 679: Lucky Kitty
Unmarked. 6"h. $30.00 – 35.00.

Plate 680: Thom Cat
Unmarked. 10½"h. $55.00 – 60.00.
Thom Cat has been reproduced,
smaller and in a solid white glaze.

Plate 681: Cat In A Sack
Unmarked. 6"h. $16.00 – 18.00.

Plate 682: Cat
Unmarked. 4¼"h. $10.00 – 12.00.

Plate 683: Cat In A Bag
Marked "GOT." 4¾"h.
$10.00 – 12.00.

Plate 684: Rabbit
Unmarked. 7"h.
$12.00 – 15.00.

Plate 685: Rabbit
Unmarked. 6¾"h. $15.00 – 18.00.

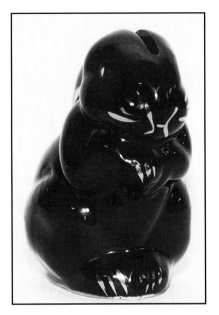

Plate 686: Rabbit
Unmarked. 5¾"h. Gold
trimmed. $45.00 – 50.00.

Plate 687: Standing Pig
Unmarked. 12"l. x 7"h. Gold trimmed. $80.00 – 85.00.

Plate 688: Sitting Pig
Unmarked. 4"h. $20.00 – 22.00.

Plate 689: Standing Pig
Marked "791." 4½"h. $40.00 – 45.00.

Plate 690: Sitting Pig
Unmarked. 7"h. $30.00 – 35.00.

Plate 691: Mother Seal With Babies
Unmarked. 5"h. $22.00 – 24.00.

Plate 692: Standing Pig
Unmarked. 11½"l. x 6"h. $65.00 – 70.00.

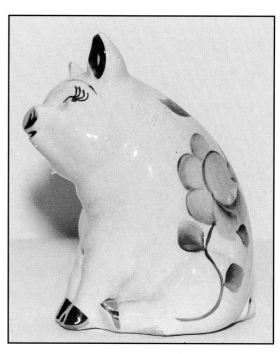

Plate 693: Sitting Pig
Unmarked. 7½"h. $60.00 – 65.00.

Plate 694: Standing Pig
Unmarked. 9"l. x 4½"h. $40.00 – 45.00.

Plate 695: Pig With Top Hat
Unmarked. 8½"h. $40.00 – 45.00.

Plate 696: Pig With Cork In Hat
Unmarked. 4½"h.
$30.00 – 35.00.

Plate 697: Standing Pig
Unmarked. Alabama Space
& Rocket Center. 3"h.
$12.00 – 15.00.

Plate 698: Standing Pig
Unmarked. Missouri The
Cave State. 2¾"h.
$12.00 – 15.00.

Plate 699: Hippopotamus
Unmarked. 4½"h. $18.00 – 20.00.

Plate 700: Spotted Hippo
Unmarked. 4¼"h. $18.00 – 20.00.

Plate 701: Flowered Hippo
Unmarked. 4¾"h. $18.00 – 20.00.

Plate 702: Fish
Unmarked. 5½"l. x 3"h. $18.00 – 20.00.

Plate 703: Goodyear Blimp
Unmarked. 4"h. $65.00 – 70.00.

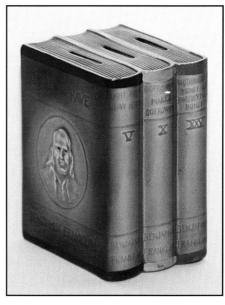

Plate 704: Ben Franklin Books
Unmarked. $40.00 – 45.00.

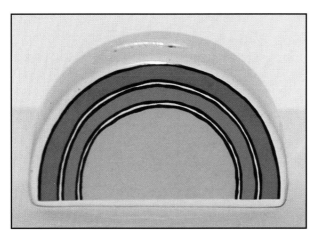

Plate 705: Rainbow
Unmarked. 3"h. $12.00 – 15.00.

Plate 707: Flask
Unmarked. 8"h. $15.00 – 18.00.

Plate 706: Scrubbing Bubbles
Marked "Scrubbing Bubbles Bank."
4¾"h. $20.00 – 22.00. This bank was
a mail-in premium.

Plate 708: Hershey Kiss
Unmarked. 4¼"h.
$22.00 – 24.00.

Plate 709: Baby Bottle
Unmarked. 7¼"h.
$15.00 – 18.00.

Plate 710: Little Sprout
Unmarked. 8¼"h. $50.00 – 55.00.

Plate 711: Lump of Coal
Unmarked. 7¼"h. $18.00 – 20.00.

Plate 712: Telephone
Unmarked. 8¼"h. $35.00 – 40.00.

Plate 713: Pot Belly Stove
Unmarked. 6½"h. $18.00 – 20.00.

Plate 714: Shoe House
Unmarked. 6½"h. $24.00 – 26.00.

Plate 715: Juke Box
Unmarked. 7"h. $22.00 – 24.00.

Plate 716: Log Cabin
Unmarked. 3¾"h. $22.00 – 24.00.

Plate 717: For Something To Wear
Unmarked. 7"h. $22.00 – 24.00.

Plate 718: Masked Lady
Unmarked. 5"h. $20.00 – 22.00.

Plate 719: Snowman
Unmarked. 6"h. $20.00 – 22.00.

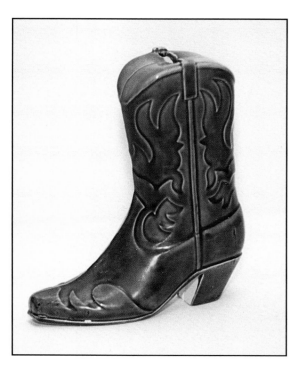

Plate 720: Cowboy Boot
Unmarked. 6¼"h. $15.00 – 18.00.

Plate 721: Pan With Handle
Unmarked. 3¼"h. $12.00 – 15.00.

Plate 722: Soccer Ball
Unmarked. 4¼"h. $20.00 – 22.00.

Plate 723: Cat
Marked "Pat. Applied For."
7"h. $40.00 – 45.00.

Plate 724: Raggedy Andy
Unmarked. 7½"h. $40.00 – 45.00.

Plate 725: Dog
Unmarked. 6"h. $40.00 – 45.00.

Distributed by Enesco.

Plate 726: Snoopy On A Watermelon
Marked "Snoopy 1958, 1963 United Feature
Synd." 4½"h. $40.00 – 45.00.

Plate 727: Snoopy and Train
Marked "Snoopy ©1959, 1966 United Feature
Syndicate, Inc." 8¼"h. $40.00 – 45.00.

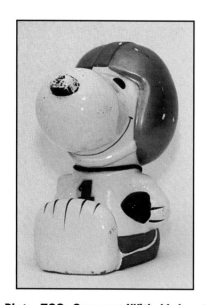

Plate 728: Snoopy With Helmet
Marked "Snoopy 1158, 1966 United
Feature Synd." 4¼"h. $40.00 – 45.00.

Plate 729: Snoopy and Woodstock
Marked "Peanuts Characters 1958, 1966, 1972
United Feature Syndicate, Inc." 8"h.
$50.00 – 55.00.

**Plate 730: Snoopy On
Dog House**
Marked "Snoopy Corp. ©1958,
1966 United Syndicate Inc." 6"h.
$40.00 – 45.00.

Plate 731: Howdy Doody TV
Paper label "Vandor Made in
Japan." 8¾"h.
$90.00 – 95.00.

Plate 732: Howdy Doody
Paper label "Made in Japan." 4½"h.
$40.00 – 45.00.

Plate 733: Juke Box
Paper label "Vandor 1985 Made in Japan."
5"h. $30.00 – 35.00.

Plate 734: Fred Flintstone
Paper label "Vandor 1989 Made in
Korea." 8¼"h. $80.00 – 85.00.

Plate 735: Mona Lisa
Marked "Vandor 1992 Made in Sri Lanka."
8"h. $30.00 – 35.00.

Plate 736: Baseball
Paper label "Vandor Made in Japan."
6"h. $35.00 – 40.00.

Plate 737: Betty Boop On Building
Marked "Made in Japan Inc. ©1981 KFS."
7¾"h. $50.00 – 55.00.

Plate 738: Betty Boop
Paper label "Vandor Made in
Sri Lanka © 1990 KFS." 5¼"h. $50.00 – 55.00.

Plate 739: Betty Boop On TV
Paper label "Vandor Made in Japan © 1986
KFS." 4"h. $45.00 – 50.00.

Plate 740: Betty Boop On Jukebox
Paper label "Vandor Made in Japan."
5¾"h. $45.00 – 50.00.

Plate 741: Sweetpea
Marked "© 1980 King Feature Syndicate,
Inc." 6¼" $125.00 – 130.00.

Plate 742: Popeye
Marked "© 1980 King Feature Syndicate."
6½"h. $125.00 – 130.00.

Plate 743: Full Figure Popeye
Marked "© King Feature Syndicate,
Inc." 7¼"h. $100.00 – 110.00.

Plate 744: Christmas Moola
Unmarked. 7"h. $25.00 – 28.00.

Plate 745: Alligator
Marked "Inc. Vandor." 3½"h. $22.00 – 24.00.

Imported from England.

Plate 746: Cow
Marked "Wade England." 5½"h. $70.00 – 75.00.

Plate 747: Frog
Marked "Wade England." 5"h. $70.00 – 75.00.

Plate: 748: Pig
Marked "Wade England." 4½"h. $70.00 – 75.00.

Plate 749: Rabbit
Marked "Wade England." 7"h. $70.00 – 75.00

Plate 750: Father Pig
Marked "Wade England." 7½"h.
$80.00 – 85.00.

Plate 751: Mother Pig
Marked "Wade England." 7"h.
$80.00 – 85.00.

Plate 752: Brother Pig
Marked "Wade England." 7¼"h.
$80.00 – 85.00.

Plate 753: Sister Pig
Marked "Wade England." 6¼"h.
$80.00 – 85.00.

Plate 754: Baby Pig
Marked "Wade England." 5½"h. $80.00 – 85.00.

Walt Disney banks, consistent with all Disney items, are a favorite with bank collectors. Over the years many companies have been licensed to produce Walt Disney products. Early items can be found marked "Walt Disney Enterprises." Later items are found marked "Walt Disney Production," items produced after 1984 will be found marked "Walt Disney Company," and the newest items are found marked "© Disney."

The banks in this section are grouped either by their producing company or exporting country.

Thumper On Block is shown in the Sigma Section. Figaro With Suspenders is shown in the American Bisque Section.

Brechner

Plate 755: Mickey Mouse
Marked "© Walt Disney Productions 22-WD-10."
6"h. $300.00 – 325.00.

Plate 756: Donald Duck
Marked "© Walt Disney Productions 22-WD-10." 6½"h. $300.00 – 325.00.

Both of these banks also have a paper label which says: "Original Dan Brechner Exclusive."

China

Plate 757: Dopey
Marked "© Disney China." 7½"h. $25.00 – 28.00.

Plate 758: Winnie The Pooh
Marked "© Walt Disney Productions." 6"h.
$35.00 – 40.00.

Plate 759: Winnie The Pooh With Honey Pot
Marked "© Disney Made in China." 7¾"h. $30.00 – 35.00.

Plate 760: Winnie The Pooh With Three Honey Pots
Marked "© Walt Disney." 7"h. $30.00 – 35.00.

China

Plate 761: Winnie The Pooh In Chair
Marked "© Disney designed by Charpinte
China." 4½"h. $35.00 – 40.00.

Plate 762: Abu
Marked "© Disney." 7"h. $25.00 – 28.00.

Plate 763: Full Figure Mickey Mouse
Marked "Disney Made in China." 8¾"h.
$50.00 – 60.00.

Plate 764: Tigger
Marked "© Disney." 7½"h. $30.00 – 35.00.

China

Plate 766: Mrs. Potts

Plate 765: Lion King and Simba
Marked "Disney Made in China." 8¼"h.
$25.00 – 28.00.

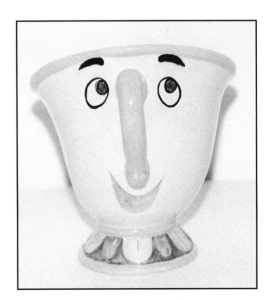

Plate 768: Chip
Marked "© Disney Made in China." 5¼"h.
$30.00 – 35.00.

Plate 767: Mrs. Potts
Marked "© Disney Made in China." 7¼"h. $45.00 – 50.00.

Enesco

Plate 769: Pocahontas
Marked "© Disney." 6¾"h.
$22.00 – 24.00.

Plate 770: Percy
Marked "© Disney." 6"h.
$22.00 – 24.00.

**Plate 771: Christmas Tree
Minnie Mouse**
Marked "© Disney." 6"h. $35.00 – 40.00.

Plate 772: Christmas Donald Duck
Marked "© Disney." 5¼"h. $35.00 – 40.00.

Enesco

Plate 773: Minnie Mouse In Car
Marked "© Disney." 5"h. $25.00 – 30.00.

Plate 774: Mickey Mouse In Car
Marked "© Disney." 4½"h. $25.00 – 30.00.

Plate 775: Christmas Mickey Mouse Head
Marked "© Disney." 6"h. $40.00 – 45.00.

Plate 776: Mickey Mouse Head
Marked "© Disney." 5¾"h. $40.00 – 45.00.

Enesco

Plate 777: Christmas Minnie Mouse Head
Marked "© Disney." 6"h. $40.00 – 45.00.

Plate 778: Minnie Mouse Head
Marked "© Disney." 6¼"h. $40.00 – 45.00.

Plate 779: Snow White
Marked "© Walt Disney Productions."
Paper label "Import Enesco Japan."
4½"h. $225.00 – 250.00.

Plate 780: Snow White
Back view.

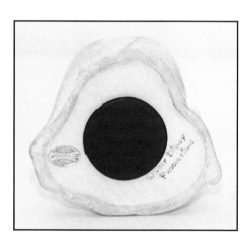

Plate 781: Snow White
Bottom view.

Hagen-Renaker

Plate 782: Figaro
Marked "Walt Disney Figaro Hagen Renaker."
5"h. $250.00 – 275.00

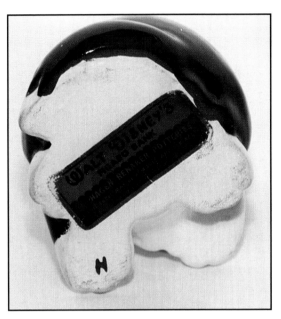

Plate 783: Figaro
Bottom view.

Japan

Plate 784: Snow White & Wishing Well
Marked "Walt Disney Prod." 5"h. $125.00 – 135.00.

Plate 785: Dalmatian
Marked "© Disney Japan." 6½"h. $18.00 – 22.00.

Korea

Plate 786: Big Al
Marked "© Walt Disney Productions."
7"h. $50.00 – 55.00.

Leeds China Company

The Leeds China Company was a distributor based in Chicago, Illinois, from 1944 to 1954. Walt Disney Productions licensed Leeds to use the Disney characters in pottery pieces. Because Leeds did not actually manufacture pottery, they bid the jobs out to pottery manufacturers, thus allowing them to obtain the best price. Leeds pottery was produced by many different pottery companies. Several companies that have been verified to have produced pottery for Leeds China Company are American Pottery Company, American Bisque, Regal China, and Ludiwici Celandon.

Plate 787: Snow White
Two different molds. The larger Snow White is marked
Keystone Dairies. The smaller Snow White is unmarked.
Larger Snow White, $150.00 – 175.00. Smaller Snow
White, $150.00 – 175.00.

Plate 788: Snow White
Bottom view.

Plate 789: Alice In Wonderland
Marked "© Walt Disney Prod." 6½"h.
$300.00 – 325.00.

Plate 790: Cinderella
Marked "Cinderella Usual Cosmetic © 1950."
6½"h. $225.00 – 250.00.

**Plate 791: Coin
Mickey Mouse**
Marked "USA Walt Disney." 6½"h.
$75.00 – 80.00.

**Plate 792: Flower
Mickey Mouse**
Marked "Mickey Mouse Walt Disney
Prod." 6½"h. $75.00 – 80.00.

Plate 793: Dumbo With Dollar Sign
"Dumbo" is inscribed on his tummy. Marked
"© Walt Disney USA Leeds." 6"h.
Gold trim. $125.00 – 130.00.

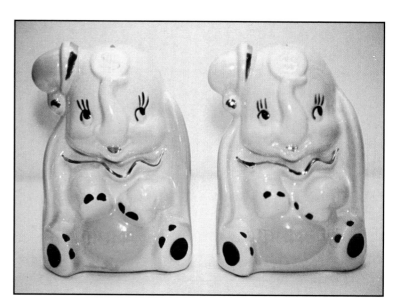

Plate 794: Dumbo With Dollar Sign
Two color variations.

Plate 795: Dumbo With Hat
Marked "Dumbo Walt Disney." 6¾"h.
Gold trim. $145.00 – 150.00.

Plate 796: Dumbo With Hat
Color variation, no gold trim.
$90.00 – 100.00.

Plate 797: Dopey

Plate 798: Dopey
Two different molds and three color variations. Large Dopey, unmarked.
Small Dopey, marked "© Walt Disney Dopey Leeds." Large Dopey,
$100.00 – 110.00. Small Dopey, $100.00 – 110.00.

Plate 799: Cowboy Mickey
Marked "Mickey Mouse Walt Disney
Prod." 6¾"h. $200.00 – 225.00.

Plate 800: Cowboy Donald
Marked "Donald Duck Walt Disney
Prod." 6¾"h. $200.00 – 225.00.

Plate 801: Donald Duck
Marked "Donald Duck Walt Disney USA." 6½"h. Gold trim,
$165.00 – 175.00. No gold, $135.00 – 140.00.

Plate 802: Coin Donald Duck
Marked "Walt Disney Prod." Cold
paint. 6"h. $100.00 – 125.00.

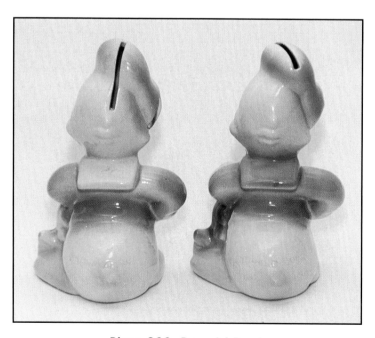

Plate 803: Donald Duck
Back view of Plate 803. Notice placement of the money slots.

Plate 804: Sitting Donald Duck
Marked "Donald Duck Walt Disney Productions." Cold paint. 8½"h. $200.00 – 225.00.

Plate 805: Standing Donald Duck
Marked "USA." 12"h. $525.00 – 550.00. This bank was original-
ly produced as a cookie jar. The head has been factory fused.

Plate 806: Standing Donald Duck
Back view.

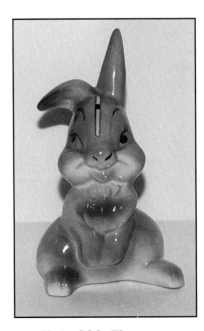

Plate 807: Pluto
Marked "© Walt Disney Prod."
6¾"h. $150.00 – 175.00.

Plate 808: Bambi
Marked "© Walt Disney Bambi."
7½"h. $150.00 – 175.00.

Plate 809: Thumper
Marked "Walt Disney Prod. Thumper."
6¾"h. $150.00 – 175.00.

London (England)

Plate 810: Donald Duck Head
Marked "Walt Disney Productions
London." 6¼"h. $300.00 – 325.00.

Plate 811: Mickey Mouse Head
Marked "Walt Disney Productions London."
6½"h. $300.00 – 325.00.

Mexico

Plate 812: Goofy Around The World
Paper label "Made in Mexico." 6"h. $30.00 – 35.00.

**Plate 813: Ludwig Von
Drake With Money Sack**
Marked "© Disney Mexico." 5"h. $50.00 – 55.00.

Schmid

Currently a licensed distributor for Walt Disney Productions.

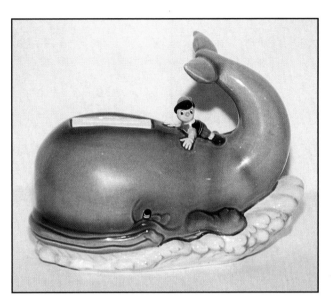

Plate 814: Pinocchio On The Whale
Coin activated musical bank. Paper label "Walt Disney Pinocchio
Hand Painted Schmid Company." 4½"h. $55.00 – 60.00.

Plate 815: Lucifer
Marked "Schmid Cinderella Hand Painted
Schmid Walt Disney." 3½"h. $25.00 – 30.00.

Plate 816: Mrs. Potts
Paper label "Beauty And The Beast; Handpainted The
Walt Disney Company." 5¼"h. $25.00 – 30.00.

Taiwan

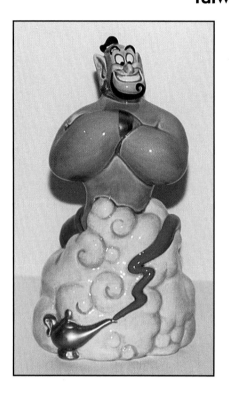

Plate 817: Genie
Marked "© Disney Taiwan." 8½"h.
$25.00 – 30.00.

Treasure Craft

Plate 818: Mrs. Potts
Marked "Treasure Craft © Disney USA."
6¾"h. $40.00 – 45.00.

Plate 819: Big Al
Marked, "© Walt Disney." 8"h. $65.00 – 75.00.

Plate 820: Hillbilly Band
Marked "Treasure Craft Walt Disney Productions Made In USA." 4"h. $80.00 – 85.00.

Unknown Maker

Plate 821: Enesco Mickey Mouse
Marked "Walt Disney Productions."
5¼"h. $250.00 – 275.00.

Plate 822: Uncle Scrooge
Marked "1961 Walt Disney Productions."
4¼"h. $100.00 – 110.00.

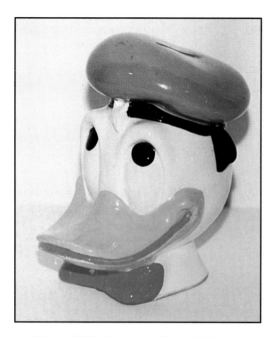

Plate 823: Enesco Donald Duck
Marked "Walt Disney Prod."
5½"h. $125.00 – 130.00.

Plate 824: Donald Duck
Marked "Walt Disney Productions." 6"h.
Cold paint. $125.00 – 130.00.

WARNER BROTHERS

**Plate 825: Bugs Bunny
With Bag Of Carrots**
Marked "© Warner Bros. Inc. 1981."
5½"h. $50.00 – 55.00.

Plate 826: Porky Pig
Marked "© Warner Bros.
Inc." 8"h. $45.00 – 50.00.

Plate 827: Wakko
Marked "TM 8 © 95 WB Made In
China." 8½"h. $30.00 – 35.00.

Plate 828: Animania Tower
Paper label "Made In China."
12½"h. $35.00 – 40.00.

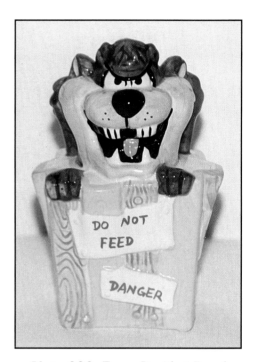

Plate 829: Taz – Do Not Feed
Paper label "Applause ©
Warner Bros. Inc. 1988 Made In Taiwan."
6"h. $45.00 – 50.00.

Plate 830: Taz and Tower
Marked "TM © 94 WB Made In Thailand." 8¼"h. $30.00 – 35.00.

Plate 831: Sylvester, Tweety, and Jukebox
Marked "TM 8 © WB 94 Made In China." 5"h. $35.00 – 40.00.

Plate 832: Daffy Duck Safe Co.
Marked paper label "Warner Bros. Inc. 1989 The Good Company; City Of Industry, Ca. 91749 Made In Taiwan." 7"h. $75.00 – 80.00.

Plate 833: Sylvester and Birdcage
Marked "TM © WB." 6¼"h. $75.00 – 80.00.

Plate 834: Daffy Duck and Money Bags
Marked "TM © 95 WB." 6"h. $30.00 – 35.00.

Plate 835 & 836: That's All Folks
Marked "© Warner Bros. Inc. 1989 Applause Inc. All Rights Reserved." 7¾"h. $100.00 – 110.00.

Bibliography

DeBolt, Gerald. *American Pottery Marks*, Collector Books, P. O. Box 3009, Paducah, Kentucky 42002-3009.

Duke, Harvey. *Official Price Guide To Pottery And Porcelain*, Eighth Edition, House of Collectibles, 201 East 50th Street, New York, NY 10022.

Giacomini, Mary Jane. *American Bisque, Collector's Guide With Prices*, Schiffer Publishing Ltd., 77 Lower Valley Road, Atglen, PA 19310.

Hull, Joan Gray. *Hull The Heavenly Pottery*, Creative Printing, 173 Second S. W., Huron, SD 57350.

Huxford, Sharon and Bob. *The Collector's Encyclopedia of Roseville Pottery*, Collector Books, P. O. Box 3009, Paducah, Kentucky 42002-3009.

Huxford, Sharon and Bob. *The Collector's Encyclopedia of Roseville Pottery*, Second Series, Collector Books, P. O. Box 3009, Paducah, KY 42002-3009.

Kovel, Ralph and Terry. *The Kovel's American Art Pottery*, Crown Publishers, Inc. 201 East 50th Street, New York, NY 10022.

Kovel, Ralph and Terry. *The Kovel's Collector's Guide To American Art Pottery*, Crown Publishers, 201 East 50th Street, New York, NY 10022.

Lehner, Lois. *U. S. Marks On Pottery, Porcelain & Clay*, Collector Books, P. O. Box 3009, Paducah, Kentucky 42002-3009.

Mangus, Jim and Bev. *Shawnee Pottery, An Identification & Value Guide*, Collector Books, P. O. Box 3009, Paducah, Kentucky 42002-3009.

Sanford, Martha and Steve. *The Guide To Brush-McCoy Pottery*, Martha and Steve Sanford, 230 Harrison Ave., Campbell, CA 95008.

Supnick, Mark & Ellen. *The Wonderful World of Cookie Jars*, L-W Book Sales, P. O. Box 69, Gas City, IN 46933.

Piece	Description	Company	Plate	Page	Price
Cat	Sitting, cold paint	LePere Pottery	365	98	$25.00-30.00
Cat	Sitting	LePere Pottery	366	98	$35.00-40.00
Cat	Kittens on a Barrel	McCoy Pottery	382	103	$25.00-30.00
Cat	Head	Japan	314	86	$25.00-30.00
Cat	With Bow	Japan	317	86	$20.00-24.00
Cat	Sitting, gold trim	LePere Pottery	367	99	$40.00-45.00
Cat	Lucky Kitty	Unknown	678	169	$30.00-35.00
Cat	Sitting	Unknown	723	179	$40.00-45.00
Cat	Fluffy	APCO	14	10	$40.00-45.00
Cat	Persian	Unknown	678	169	$18.00-20.00
Cat	Sitting, Padlock	Japan	264	75	$45.00-50.00
Cat	Fluffy	APCO	15, 16	10	$40.00-45.00
Cat	Sitting	Unknown	682	170	$10.00-12.00
Cat	Turnabout	Holt Howard	233	66	$70.00-75.00
Cat	In Airplane	Unknown	676	169	$25.00-28.00
Cat	Cheshire	Fitz & Floyd	213	60	$55.00-60.00
Cat	Feed The Kitty	ABC/APCO	18	10	$95.00-100.00 ea.
Cat	Sitting, Padlock	Japan	255	73	$40.00-45.00
Cat	Fluffy	APCO	17	11	$40.00-45.00
Cat	House, Padlock	NAPCO	484	125	$30.00-32.00
Cat	Figaro	ABC/APCO	19	11	$100.00-125.00
Cat	Padlock	NAPCO	479	124	$40.00-45.00
Cat	Kliban	Sigma	553	142	$60.00-65.00
Cat	Coal Bucket	McCoy Pottery	401	107	$55.00-60.00
Cat	In a Sack	Unknown	681	170	$16.00-18.00
Cat	Thom	Unknown	680	170	$55.00-60.00
Cat	In a Bag	Unknown	683	170	$10.00-12.00
Cat	With Bow	Unknown	677	169	$25.00-30.00
Cat	Fluffy	APCO	14	10	$40.00-45.00
Cat	Sitting	Miscellaneous	427	113	$30.00-35.00
Charlie Tuna	On a Can	Miscellaneous	456	119	$75.00-80.00
Chef	Black	Miscellaneous	462	120	$20.00-22.00
Chef	Entenmann's	Unknown	640	162	$45.00-50.00
Chest	Treasure	Terrace Ceramics	556	144	$80.00-85.00
Chest	Money Chest	McCoy Pottery	380	102	$65.00-70.00
Chewbacca	Standing	Sigma	548	142	$75.00-80.00
Chick	Standing	Lefton	341	92	$40.00-45.00
Chick	Chick With Bow	ABC/APCO	87	25	$45.00-50.00
Chick	Standing, With Hat	Miscellaneous	416	111	$22.00-26.00
Chick	Standing	Diamond Pottery Co.	172	48	$35.00-40.00
Chic Pottery				45	
Chicken	Chicken Feed	Royal Copley	514	133	$40.00-45.00
Chinese	Nodder	Japan	279	79	$40.00-45.00
Chip	Tea Cup	Walt Disney	768	189	$30.00-35.00
Cinderella	Standing	Walt Disney	790	195	$225.00-250.00
Cleminsons				47	
Clock	Tower, The Williamsburg	McCoy Pottery	393	105	$25.00-30.00
Clown	With Top Hat	Sierra Vista Ceramics	547	141	$30.00-35.00
Clown	With Patches	Unknown	622	158	$20.00-22.00
Clown	Head	Unknown	623	159	$25.00-30.00
Clown	Head, Padlock	Japan	267	76	$40.00-45.00
Clown	Head	Japan	276	78	$20.00-25.00
Clown	On Base	Unknown	625	159	$65.00-70.00
Clown	Standing With Balloons	Enesco	186	52	$20.00-25.00

Piece	Description	Company	Plate	Page	Price
Dog	Hound	Unknown	650	164	$20.00-25.00
Dog	Puppy, Gold Trim	LePere Pottery	351	95	$40.00-45.00
Dog	Ford	Miscellaneous	448	118	$45.00-50.00
Dog	Pekingese	Shawnee Pottery (new)	532	138	$33.33
Dog	For Bills I Can't Forget	Japan	272	77	$25.00-30.00
Dog	Head	Brush	143	40	$45.00-50.00
Dog	Rover	Brush	144	40	$30.00-35.00
Dog	Running Puppy	Maddux of California	372	100	$75.00-80.00
Dog	Sitting, Padlock	Japan	256	73	$40.00-45.00
Dog	Lucky Penny Puppy	McCoy Pottery	404	108	$15.00-20.00
Dog	Spaniel	APCO	34	14	$45.00-50.00
Dog	Hound, Dresser Caddy	McCoy Pottery	403	107	$35.00-40.00
Dog	Fi - Dough	Japan	270	76	$30.00-35.00
Dog	Sitting, Padlock Poodle	Japan	265	75	$45.00-50.00
Dog	Nipper	Miscellaneous	437	115	$25.00-30.00
Donald Duck	Head	Walt Disney	810	200	$300.00-325.00
Donald Duck	With Fish	Walt Disney	801	198	$135.00-140.00
Donald Duck	Cowboy	Walt Disney	800	197	$200.00-225.00
Donald Duck	Head	Walt Disney	824	204	$125.00-130.00
Donald Duck	Standing With Coin	Walt Disney	802	198	$100.00-125.00
Donald Duck	Dan Brechner	Walt Disney	756	186	$300.00-325.00
Donald Duck	Sitting With Coin	Walt Disney	804	198	$200.00-225.00
Donald Duck	Christmas Toy Bag	Walt Disney	772	190	$35.00-40.00
Donald Duck	Head	Walt Disney	825	204	$125.00-130.00
Donald Duck	Standing With Bow Tie	Walt Disney	805	199	$525.00-550.00
Donald Duck	With Fish, gold trim	Walt Disney	801	198	$135.00-140.00
Donkey	Standing With Saddle	Diamond Pottery Co.	171	48	$35.00-40.00
Donkey	Donkey on Base	ABC/APCO	72	22	$65.00-70.00
Dopey	Sitting	Walt Disney	757	187	$25.00-28.00
Dopey	Standing	Walt Disney	798	197	$100.00-110.00 ea.
Dorothy	Standing	Miscellaneous	439	116	$85.00-90.00
Dracula	Black Cape	Fitz & Floyd	214	60	$130.00-135.00
Dryer		Miscellaneous	438	115	$50.00-55.00
Duck	Standing	Japan	312	85	$25.00-30.00
Duck	Artist	Miscellaneous	442	117	$26.00-28.00
Dumbo	With Hat, gold trim	Walt Disney	795	196	$145.00-150.00
Dumbo	With $ Sign & Hat, gold trim	Walt Disney	793	196	$125.00-130.00
Dumbo	With Hat	Walt Disney	796	196	$90.00-100.00
Eagle	Wings Up	McCoy Pottery	399	106	$45.00-50.00
Eagle	Wings Down	McCoy Pottery	400	107	$30.00-35.00
Egg	Mailman	Miscellaneous	430	113	$22.00-24.00
Elephant	Standing, gold trim	LePere Pottery	362	98	$40.00-45.00
Elephant	Sitting	Unknown	666	167	$15.00-18.00
Elephant	Sitting	ABC/APCO	86	25	$30.00-35.00
Elephant	Standing	Unknown	669	168	$18.00-20.00
Elephant	Lying on Back	Unknown	667	167	$15.00-18.00
Elephant	Standing Elephant on Base	ABC/APCO	67	21	$55.00-65.00
Elephant	Dancing on Base	ABC/APCO	68	21	$65.00-75.00
Elephant	Sitting, gold trim	LePere Pottery	348	94	$40.00-45.00
Elephant	Rocking	Unknown	668	167	$22.00-24.00
Elephant	Sitting, cold paint	LePere Pottery	349	94	$25.00-30.00
Elephant	Sitting	Unknown	664	166	$22.00-24.00
Elephant	Sitting, I Love Atlantic	Unknown	665	167	$18.00-20.00
Elephant	Happy Elephant	ABC/APCO	58	19	$55.00-60.00

Piece	Description	Company	Plate	Page	Price
Globe	For My Trip	Japan	319	87	$25.00-28.00
Goebel Art				62	
Gonder Art Pottery				64	
Goofy	Around The World	Walt Disney	812	200	$30.00-35.00
Grandma	With Glasses	Unknown	599	153	$22.00-25.00
Grimace	Standing	Miscellaneous	458	119	$45.00-50.00
Harley Davidson	Gas Tank	Unknown	612	156	$40.00-45.00
Harley Davidson	Gas Tank	Unknown	610	156	$125.00-150.00
Harley Davidson	Gas Tank	Unknown	609	156	$85.00-90.00
Harley Davidson	Gas Tank	Unknown	608	155	$45.00-50.00
Harley Davidson	Gas Tank	Unknown	611	156	$65.00-70.00
Hat	Confederate	Unknown	620	158	$18.00-20.00
Hershey Chocolate	Hershey Chef	Unknown	626	159	$65.00-70.00
Hershey Kiss		Unknown	708	176	$22.00-24.00
Hillbilly	In A Barrel	Twin Winton	570	147	$125.00-150.00
Hillbilly	Sitting With Jug	Unknown	634	160	$20.00-22.00
Hillbilly Band	Round	Walt Disney	820	203	$80.00-85.00
Hippo	Spotted	Unknown	700	174	$18.00-20.00
Hippo	Sitting	NAPCO	480	124	$25.00-30.00
Hippo	Standing Flowered	Unknown	701	174	$18.00-20.00
Hippopotamus	Lying Down	Unknown	699	174	$18.00-20.00
Hobo	Standing	Treasure Craft	560	145	$60.00-65.00
Hobo	Head	Brush	147	41	$75.00-80.00
Hobo	Standing	Unknown	637	161	$75.00-80.00
Hobo	Standing	Unknown	638	161	$75.00-80.00
Holt Howard				65	
Horse	Rocking	Unknown	668	167	$22.00-24.00 ea.
Horse	Rocking	Treasure Craft	559	144	$70.00-75.00
Horse	Rocking	Pearl China Co.	495	128	$45.00-50.00
Hot Air Balloon	Coming out of City	Louisville Stoneware	371	100	$55.00-60.00
Hotei	Standing	Twin Winton	589	150	$55.00-60.00
House	Cookie Bank	McCoy Pottery	379	102	$140.00-150.00
House	Bear Watering Flowers	Enesco	201	56	$25.00-30.00
Howdy Doody	In TV	Vandor	731	181	$90.00-95.00
Howdy Doody	Head	Vandor	732	181	$40.00-45.00
Howdy Doody	Bob Smith	Shawnee Pottery Co	525	136	$500.00-550.00
Hubert Lion	Standing	Lefton	340	92	$110.00-125.00
Hull Pottery Co.				67	
Human Bean	Tennis Racket	Enesco	178	50	$35.00-40.00
Human Bean	Sunbathing With Newspaper	Enesco	184	52	$35.00-40.00
Human Bean	Bowling Ball	Enesco	179	50	$35.00-40.00
Human Bean	Sunbathing	Enesco	177	50	$35.00-40.00
Human Bean	Money Bag	Enesco	176	50	$35.00-40.00
Human Bean	Ball Bat	Enesco	185	52	$35.00-40.00
Human Bean	Holding Dollar Bills	Enesco	180	51	$35.00-40.00
Human Bean	Christmas Cash	Enesco	182	51	$50.00-55.00
Human Bean	Santa and Baby Bean	Enesco	183	51	$65.00-70.00
Human Bean	Skis	Enesco	181	51	$35.00-40.00
Humpty Dumpty	Alice in Philcoland	ABC/APCO	56	18	$120.00-130.00
Humpty Dumpty		Corl Pottery Co.	168	47	$80.00-85.00
Humpty Dumpty	Sitting on Books	Japan	295	82	$75.00-80.00
Humpty Dumpty	Sitting on Wall	Japan	296	82	$65.00-70.00
Indian	Baseball Player	Unknown	615	157	$300.00-325.00
Indian	Head	Japan	269	76	$30.00-35.00

Piece	Description	Company	Plate	Page	Price
Pig	Standing	Unknown	687	172	$80.00-85.00
Pig	Sitting	Unknown	688	171	$20.00-22.00
Pig	For Your Rainy Day	ABC/APCO	9 – 11	9	$125.00-150.00
Pig	Formal Cookie Jar	Brush	133	37	$300.00-350.00 ea.
Pig	Sitting	Chic	162	45	$70.00-75.00
Pig	Embossed Flowers, Open Eye	ABC/APCO	113	31	$25.00-30.00
Pig	Sitting	Brush	132	37	$400.00-450.00
Pig	Standing	ABC/APCO	99	28	$45.00-50.00
Pig	Corky, Standing	Hull Pottery Co.	245	70	$110.00-115.00
Pig	Turnabout Cookie Jar, Hands in Pockets	ABC/APCO	114	32	$250.00-300.00
Pig	Standing	Beaumont Brothers	126	35	$15.00-18.00
Pig	Hands in Pocket	ABC/APCO	118	32	$250.00-300.00
Pig	Recessed Petals	ABC/APCO	96	27	$45.00-50.00
Pig	Turnabout Cookie Jar, Hands in Pockets	ABC/APCO	114	32	$250.00-300.00
Pig	Standing	Unknown	696	173	$30.00-35.00
Pig	Attitude With Bow	ABC/APCO	104	29	$85.00-90.00
Pig	Sitting	Unknown	693	172	$60.00-65.00
Pig	Brother	Wade	752	185	$80.00-85.00
Pig	Standing	Unknown	689	171	$40.00-45.00
Pig	Pig With Bow	APCO	85	25	$30.00-35.00
Pig	Standing Pig With Bow	ABC/APCO	109	30	$45.00-50.00
Pig	Attitude Pig Recessed Fruit	ABC/APCO	106	29	$85.00-90.00
Pig	Standing Pig With Bow	ABC/APCO	108	31	$55.00-65.00
Pig	Standing Pig With Indented Dots	ABC/APCO	110	30	$100.00-110.00
Pig	Diaper Pin	ABC/APCO	50	17	$350.00-375.00
Pig	Standing Pig With Indented Dots	ABC/APCO	111 – 112	31	$30.00-35.00
Pig	Embossed Clover	ABC/APCO	95	27	$100.00-110.00
Pig	Attitude With Bow	ABC/APCO	103	29	$110.00-120.00
Pig	Attitude With Bow	ABC/APCO	101	28	$100.00-110.00
Pig	Paddy Pig	APCO	94	27	$70.00-75.00
Pig	Bow Pig Color Variation	ABC/APCO	84	26	$30.00-35.00
Pig	Attitude Pig	ABC/APCO	107	29	$70.00-75.00
Pig	Sister	Wade	753	185	$80.00-85.00
Pig	With Top Hat	Royal Copley	511	132	$40.00-45.00
Pig	Mother	Wade	751	185	$80.00-85.00
Pig	Razor Back	Brush	139	39	$40.00-45.00
Pig	Standing	Wade	748	184	$70.00-75.00
Pig	Standing	Brush	149	41	$40.00-45.00
Pig	Padlock	ABC/APCO	49	17	$475.00-500.00
Pig	Winnie Cookie Jar, gold trim	Shawnee Pottery Co.	529	137	$900.00-1,000.00
Pig	Upside Down Pig on Base	ABC/APCO	71	22	$65.00-70.00
Pig	Standing	Brush	141	39	$30.00-35.00
Pig	Bow Pig, mold variation	ABC/APCO	83	24	$30.00-3500 ea.
Pig	Bow Pig	ABC/APCO	81	24	$30.00-35.00
Pig	Little Girl	APCO	73	22	$40.00-45.00
Pig	Sitting	Unknown	606	155	$18.00-20.00
Pig	Dimples	ABC/APCO	79	23	$35.00-40.00
Pig	Bedtime Pig, dress not flared, gold trim	APCO	77 – 78	23	$35.00-40.00
Pig	Indented Dot Dancing Pig	ABC/APCO	75	22	$30.00-35.00
Pig	Bedtime Pig, flared dress	APCO	76	22	$30.00-35.00
Pig	Bow Pig, mold variation	ABC/APCO	82	24	$30.00-35.00
Pig	Wall Hanger, Feet Together	Morton	474	123	$60.00-65.00
Pig	Corky, Standing	Hull Pottery Co.	244	70	$115.00-120.00
Pig	Standing, no trim, gold trim	LePere Pottery	356	96	$20.00-25.00, $40.00-45.00

Piece	Description	Company	Plate	Page	Price
Snow White	At Wishing Well	Walt Disney	784	193	$125.00-135.00
Snow White	Bird on Her Finger	Walt Disney	779	192	$225.00-250.00
Snow White	Standing Holding Dress	Walt Disney	787	194	$150.00-175.00
Snowman	Snowman With Top Hat	ABC/APCO	89	26	$65.00-70.00 ea.
Snowman	Standing	Miscellaneous	415	110	$22.00-24.00
Snowman		Unknown	719	178	$20.00-22.00
Snowman	Snowman	Japan	328	89	$30.00-35.00
Soldier	Standing, Cookie Jar	Cardinal China Co.	160	45	$500.00-550.00
Soldier	Nodder	Unknown	598	153	$45.00-50.00
Soldier	Standing	California Originals	154	43	$55.00-60.00
Spaceship	Spaceship	ABC/APCO	57	18	$75.00-80.00
Spaceship	Flat Gold	NAPCO	477	124	$200.00-210.00
Speedboat	Man in Boat	Enesco	202	56	$25.00-30.00
Squirrel	Squirrel With Nut on Base	ABC/APCO	69, 70	21	$45.00-50.00
Squirrel	Sitting, Tongue Moves	Japan	313	85	$45.00-50.00
Squirrel	Sitting	California Originals	155	43	$55.00-60.00
Squirrel	Sitting Holding a Nut	Twin Winton	577	148	$45.00-50.00
Squirrel	Sitting	Goebel Art	222	63	$65.00-70.00
Squirrel	Sitting	Shawnee Pottery (new)	536	139	$33.33
Squirrel	Sitting	Pearl China Co.	497	129	$75.00-80.00
Squirrel	Squirrel With Nut	ABC/APCO	88	25	$25.00-30.00
Squirrel	Sitting	Sierra Vista Ceramics	541	140	$75.00-80.00
Stagecoach		Treasure Craft	563	145	$40.00-45.00
Starset				143	
Stove		Miscellaneous	438	115	$50.00-55.00
Stove	Pot Belly	Unknown	713	174	$18.00-20.00
Superman	Standing	Miscellaneous	450	118	$600.00-800.00
Superman	Head	Enesco	192	54	$100.00-110.00
Swan	Swan	ABC	37	14	$45.00-50.00
Sweet Pea	Sweet Pea	ABC/APCO	38	15	$1,500.00+
Sweet Pea	Full Body	Vandor	741	183	$125.00-130.00
Sylvester	Tweety in Bird Cage	Warner Brothers	833	206	$75.00-80.00
Sylvester	Tweety and Jukebox	Warner Brothers	831	205	$35.00-40.00
Taz	Do Not Feed	Warner Brothers	829	205	$45.00-50.00
Taz	Holding Tower	Warner Brothers	830	205	$30.00-35.00
Telephone		Japan	318	86	$30.00-35.00
Telephone		Unknown	712	176	$35.00-40.00
Telephone	Telephone With Flowers	ABC/APCO	93	26	$30.00-35.00
Terrace Ceramics				143	
The Little Texan	The Little Texan	Hull Pottery Co.	252	72	$600.00-650.00
Thrifty Tom	Save for Rainy Day	McCoy Pottery	385	103	$30.00-35.00
Thumper	Sitting	Walt Disney	809	199	$150.00-175.00
Tigger	Hidden Treasure	Walt Disney	764	188	$30.00-35.00
Tinman	Wizard of Oz	Enesco	174	49	$75.00-80.00
Tinman	Standing	Miscellaneous	439	116	$85.00-90.00
Tom Cat	With House	Miscellaneous	457	119	$45.00-50.00
Tom and Jerry	On a Box	Miscellaneous	440	116	$75.00-80.00
Toy Shop	Santa	Enesco	191	53	$35.00-40.00
Train	Santa	Japan	329	89	$35.00-40.00
Train	Thomas	Schmid	522	135	$30.00-35.00
Train	With Conductor	Unknown	639	162	$25.00-28.00
Treasure Craft				144	
Tree	Christmas Tree	Japan	327	89	$30.00-35.00
Troll	Norfin	Miscellaneous	426	113	$45.00-50.00